# Growing Up in a Shipyard

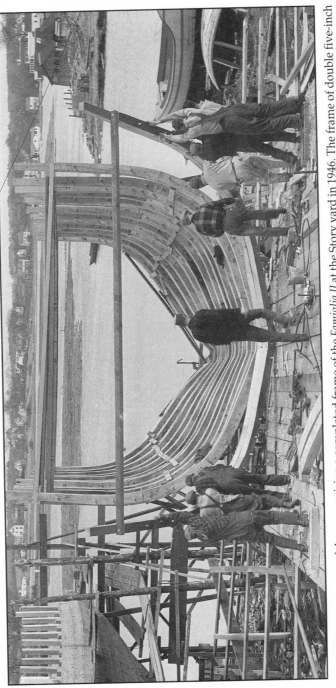

1. Here we see part of the gang raising a completed frame of the *Famiglia II* at the Story yard in 1946. The frame of double five-inch timbers, fastened with galvanized carriage bolts, has been assembled on the framing stage in the foreground, and at the cry "frame up!" all in the vicinity have come to assist the framing gang in lifting it into place. Some of the pieces for the next frame—futtocks—are lying at the forward edge of the stage. The frames assembled as complete U-shaped units and erected across the keel like this are the "square frames." Beyond the vessel is a good view of the upper Essex River at high tide with the little marsh island out there. At right is the sawmill building of the James shipyard, and in the distance are the houses of the Water Street area of South Essex. *(Photo by author.)*

# Growing Up in a Shipyard

*Reminiscences of a Shipbuilding Life
in Essex, Massachusetts*

By Dana A. Story

Mystic Seaport Museum, Inc.
Mystic, Connecticut

in association with

The Essex Shipbuilding Museum, Inc.
Essex, Massachusetts
1991

**To Margaret,
my secure anchor to windward
when the seas were rough**

Copyright 1991 by Mystic Seaport Museum, Inc.
All rights reserved

Cataloging in Publication Data

Story, Dana A., 1919-
      Growing up in a shipyard: reminiscences of a shipbuilding life in
      Essex, Massachusetts.
Mystic, Conn., Mystic, Seaport Museum, Inc., 1991
      1. Essex, Mass. — Hist.
      2. Shipbuilding — Mass. — Essex
      3. Story, Dana A., 1919-
      I. Title

F74.E7S85

ISBN: 0-913372-57-9

Designed by Terry A. Rutledge
Typeset in Palatino
Printed by Thomson-Shore, Inc., Dexter, Michigan

Manufactured in the United States of America

# Contents

# Illustrations

# Foreword

Fifteen years ago, on the opening day of the Essex Shipbuilding Museum in Essex, Massachusetts, Luther T. Burnham, caulker, cut a red, white, and blue silk ribbon stretched across the museum doorway. Looking on were the handful of Essex shipbuilders left who once worked in the big shipyards of Essex: Albert Doucette, Leo Doyle, Johnnie James, Wendell Lufkin, Dana Story, and George Story (no relation). They each in turn cut a length of ribbon. Today, nearly the last of the Essex shipbuilders, Dana Adams Story is the town's official historian, and one of the greatest assets of the Essex Shipbuilding Museum.

Twice president of the Essex Historical Society, Dana has also served on the museum steering committee. As a museum historian he is relied on to advise us as well as to answer questions, identify photographs, and research texts. A collection of 100 glass negatives taken in the Essex shipyards by his uncle, Edwin Story, was acquired by purchase this year, and Dana was essential to their proper identification, as he has been with all photographs in the museum collections. He, himself, has contributed hundreds of photographs and negatives, which form the Story Photographic Collection within the museum archives.

A new museum exhibit replicating two frame sections of the 1900 fishing schooner *Rob Roy*, from keelson to waterline, in full scale, would have been impossible without Dana's help. The tools exhibited with the frames are "yard tools" from the Story yard contributed by Dana. These tools were most likely used in the construction of the original *Rob Roy* and were used by our staff to build the exhibit. The lines for the *Rob Roy* came from a large collection of plans also given by Dana.

With Dana's assistance, and by his example, a nucleus of plans, photographs, models, tools, and documents in the museum archives has grown in the last 15 years and now includes information on every known vessel built in the Essex shipyards. It is indeed a pleasure to be able to work with the rich resource the museum collections have become; it is a privilege to be able to work with Dana.

The Essex-built schooners *Lettie G. Howard*, *L. A. Dunton*, and *Evelina M. Goulart* from the Story shipyard, and *Ernestina* ex-*Effie M. Morrissey*, *Roseway*, *Pilot*, and *Adventure* from the James shipyard survive today, as does the dragger *St. Rosalie* from the Jonathan Story shipyard. With Dana's help the Essex Shipbuilding Museum continues to grow and improve as a resource for the maintenance and interpretation of these vessels and for all those built in Essex, and to foster an appreciation of the 350 years of shipbuilding in this town.

With his candor in writing this book, we are better able to appreciate the measure of the man who has helped invigorate this history and allow us to make it ours, whoever we are, wherever we are. We are indebted to Mystic Seaport for their commitment to this work and thank them, with Dana, for allowing us to share in this account of a shipbuilder of Essex, our patron and friend.

DIANA H. STOCKTON
*Museum Administrator*
*Essex Shipbuilding Museum*

# Preface

To be concerned with boats floating in salt water inevitably means an involvement with tides. Sooner or later, in one way or another, one has to deal with the tide and what it does. In my own case, this has meant a lifetime association. Whether working in somebody else's shipyard or my own, I have acknowledged the coming and going of the tide and geared my life's activity to it. Moreover, to be brought up and live in Essex, Massachusetts, is to acquire an especial awareness of the tide, since a great portion of the town's life and history has of necessity been, and still is, meshed with the coming and going of the salt water in the Essex River. It was high water for the launching of thousands of vessels and low water for the digging of countless barrels of soft-shelled clams. Even local farmers looked to the proper tide for the harvesting of salt hay from the hundreds of acres of marshland within the boundaries of the town. As a small child I soon learned that the vessels in my father's shipyard were launched at high tide, and since that shipyard became a place for me and my friends to play, almost from the time I could walk, I looked forward to a "boat la'nch" with great anticipation and excitement.

The lore of the tides carried over into other aspects of daily life. My mother, for example, was deathly afraid of thundershowers and, at the first rumble of thunder, would look at a tide calendar (most Essex homes had one) believing that if a storm arose on a going tide it wouldn't amount to much, but, if it arose with the tide coming, it would hang around until the tide turned. No amount of remonstrance could disabuse her of this notion.  And she was by no means alone in this manner of thinking, since many people were convinced that the tides bore some influence upon the weather.  Whether they did or not will not here be a matter of concern.  Rather, I hope to draw what may become an obvious analogy between the tides of the ocean (and the Essex River) and the tides of my own fortune.  As the tide flows in, reaches its full, and then ebbs away, so also did my hopes, my spirits, my ambition rise, reach a peak, and quietly ebb away.  At least it all made quite a splash while it was happening.

Obviously then, this is not to be a rags to riches tale, nor must it be construed in any sense that I write these pages with any feeling of self-importance or extraordinary accomplishment.  My life has been quite unremarked; I have not been a "mover and shaker"; I did not become a captain of industry, commerce, or government.  My father did well and I had three first cousins who, starting from nothing, became millionaires—one a corporate lawyer, one in commerce, and one (the most successful) an investment counselor.  Whatever it was that gave impetus to their financial success obviously eluded me.  However, I feel that in my early family life and my few years as a shipbuilder I encountered a large number of interesting and remarkable people, many of whom deserve to be mentioned.  Also, I think my family, work, and shipyard experiences have given rise to some events of interest, especially to those who are or have been concerned with wooden boats.  Further, I have attempted along the way to preserve a segment of history of a unique and historic town.

Lastly, I make no attempt with all of this to produce a "how-to" book.  I have no intention of detailing the uncounted processes in the building of a wooden ship.  Others have dealt with this.  I assume on the part of the reader a modicum of general knowledge about the structure of wooden boats and will only superficially treat the various elements of those that were particular to Essex.  I merely want to describe my own involvement with it all or, more simply, tell what happened.

As a shipbuilder myself, this involvement lasted just under three years, from August 1945 to June 1948.  During this time we built seven draggers, the largest being 180 gross tons. In that brief span I managed to go, with the ebbing of my fortunes, from riches to rags—with the rags coming at a moment in history when, to all intents and purposes, wooden shipbuilding was about done anyway. I have had to depend largely on memory for such facts, figures, and dates as I have used, since what had been my office in the old shop was destroyed by fire in June of 1950, taking with it all written records of the Arthur D. Story Shipyard, Inc. Fortunately, I had a fine collection of photographs which were not destroyed, and these have been of invaluable help in preparing this manuscript. Also, I have been assisted in my recollection by two men who were there with me and who have gladly given their help. For this I am grateful.

The term "growing up" can be a rather subjective one. The obvious connotation refers to the physical, mental, and emotional development of a child from birth to adulthood. Another common application of the term deals with the maturing of an individual in the areas of experience and wisdom. It is this latter meaning that, I think, more properly describes the sequence of events herein related. It was my original intention to entitle this manuscript "Ebb Tide," for reasons stated above. However, upon reflection it seemed that "Growing Up in a Shipyard" was a better choice for two reasons: first, the title is literally applied in chapter 1, "20 Winthrop St.," my father's house, where I spent my boyhood from infancy to teen-age; second, I hope that throughout the remaining chapters it will become apparent to the reader that from an experiential and emotional point of view, the title continues to apply as I encounter viscissitudes of my career leading up to chapter 8, a period in which I do, indeed, continue to "grow up." I might now add that my growing up (in that sense) continued until the day of my retirement.

In conclusion, I wish to acknowledge the help given by Albert Doucette and Wendell Lufkin who were there with me in my shipyard; also, to thank my friends Greg Gibson of the Ten Pound Island Book Company, Philip Thiel, and Philip C. Bolger for their editorial suggestions and comments.

# Introduction

I cannot begin an account of my own experience as a builder of wooden ships without first giving the reader a brief account of the remarkable history of the shipbuilding industry in our little Massachusetts town of Essex or, in short, how things got to where they were when I came along. This was a period of some 260 years, more or less.

As nearly as we can determine, wooden shipbuilding in Essex had its beginning in the 1650s. The first sawmill was built at that time, and it is assumed that some of the products of the mill went into boat construction. At any rate, we do know that by 1668 enough shipbuilding was going on to warrant setting aside an area of common land on the river bank at the center of town to be used for the building of vessels. What is now Essex was at that time known as Chebacco Parish in the town of Ipswich, and it remained "Chebacco" until it separated from the mother town in February 1819.

The settlers here, the first of whom arrived in 1634, found it to be a hardscrabble existence what with the enveloping forest underlaid with much ledge and a predominately clay soil. All was interlaced with rocks and boulders. The miles of stone walls that even today encircle all the old plots of land are a mute testimony to the brutally hard work required merely to clear the land. No wonder these people turned to the sea to help provide their food. To do this only required a boat, so they taught themselves to build boats. A supply of lumber was no problem–there it was, ready for the taking, both hard and soft woods. Thus was born a shipbuilding industry.

An ancient Essex tradition has it that the very first boat was built in the garret of a house in the southern part of town and that the garret window and part of the wall had to be removed to get it out. That a boat of a size to be constructed in an attic would be spoken of as "built" seems questionable. Even more questionable is the rest of the legend, which states that two Burnhams, man and boy, sailed down the coast of Maine in this boat for a fare of fish. If that's the case, the house must have been all garret or else the garret was the ground floor. But enough of this!

In due course the boats Chebacco men built became larger and heavier, enabling them to go further offshore for their fish, and also, in due course, the word got around and men began to come from the whole Cape Ann area to have their boats built by the Chebacco men. Without belaboring these points, suffice it to say that by the year 1852 there were fifteen shipyards in town and together they turned out sixty vessels. Excepting the farmers, most able-bodied men in town worked in the shipyards. It might be noted in passing that of the fifteen builders in 1852, five of them were Burnhams and five were Storys.

Let me digress for a bit to point out that in most of our shipbuilding years a "shipyard" was no more than a plot of land beside the river. The word "river" is rather loosely applied here inasmuch as our river is not a river in the strict sense of the word, but rather a tidal inlet, or estuary, which winds in through the salt marshes some four miles or more from Ipswich Bay. Essentially everything was done by hand. Sawmills did indeed produce planks and thicker timbers, but this was generally round-edge stock (bark still on two edges), and all other shaping operations were done by hand. Every workman provided all his own tools. A yard owner provided the few items of heavy equipment, such as C-clamps (some of which might need a man and boy just to lift), an assortment of large augurs, peaveys (cant hooks), two-man crosscut saws, a grindstone, blocks-and-falls, and the pit saw together with a shop building to house all of these and the tool chests of the men. The first steam-powered band saw in an Essex yard did not appear until 1884.

Along with shipbuilding, a number of ancillary trades or
businesses developed. First of all, perhaps, were the blacksmith shops that made the ironwork for the hull and spars–the
chainplates, deck eyes, sheet travelers, gammon irons, eye
bands for the spars, bobstay irons, etc. An ordinary blacksmith
wouldn't have done this sort of thing. Then, of course, there
was the spar yard, which produced the masts, booms, gaffs,
and bowsprits, with an occasional flagstaff or derrick for outside interests. In addition to these were shops that made
wooden pumps for the vessels, wooden tackle blocks, and the
big wooden anchor stocks. Two shops turned out the anchor
windlasses that were installed on every vessel. I must mention
the loftsmen who first laid down a vessel and then made all
the necessary molds and patterns. Near the shipyards in the
center of town was a little boatshop where the wherries carried by many vessels in the stern davits were made.

Curiously, in the early years of our history, and up to the
late 1840s, many vessels were not built in shipyards but rather
in the dooryards of the men who built them. Sometimes these
were a mile or more from the river. Obviously these were not
the large fishing schooners that came to be associated with the
work of later years but were craft of about forty feet or so in
length. When finished, these boats were loaded into sets of
wheels and pulled by teams of oxen to the river. Here they
were run down into the river bed at low water and later floated free by the incoming tide.

So we see by all of this that the fabric of life in Essex was in-
extricably linked to wooden shipbuilding and all that went
with it. To a diminishing degree this situation obtained right
up to the years immediately following World War II. My distant cousin, Lewis Story, spent much of his life gathering the
statistical record of the industry. Going back to the 1790s,
when records first began to be kept, he produced a listing of
3,300 Essex-built vessels; 1,388 of these were built in the years
from 1860 to 1980 and of these, 424 were built by my father,
Arthur D. Story. This was the greatest number of vessels ever
built by a single builder in the history of Essex shipbuilding.

When I arrived on the scene in April of 1919 there were three builders still operating: John F. James & Son (operated by Everett B. James), Owen Lantz, and Arthur D. Story. This was a lot fewer than fifteen, but the tonnage being turned out probably came close to that produced by all fifteen yards in 1852. Of the vessels on the stocks at that moment, three of them were three-masted coasting schooners, and big ones, too.

It is my hope that by all of this the reader may be made aware of the significance of the shipbuilding industry to the town of Essex. As a community we were unique in our little corner of the world. No town anywhere around us was as well known except maybe Gloucester, for whom through the years we built most of her fishing fleet even though she had shipyards of her own. Many of the products of our yards found their way to nearly every part of the globe. We were, and are, proud of that.

As a postscript, I might note that as this manuscript goes to press, I am the only one still living who can tell these stories of life in an Essex shipyard from personal experience. Every other man who worked in the old Arthur D. Story or James shipyards has now passed on.

# 1

# 20 Winthrop Street

It is difficult to think of my boyhood home without associating the place with my father. His presence dominated our home as it dominated his shipyard. I don't mean this in the sense that he was overbearing or dictatorial or arrogant; he wasn't, but at the same time Mother and I, the rest of his family and the men of his shipyard knew him to be a man of strong opinions, few words and one who fully realized he was the boss. This is not to say, either, that Mother couldn't or wouldn't express herself very positively if the occasion warranted. She also was a strong character and she too meant what she said. After all, she had been a school teacher for fifteen years before marriage. In any case, we accepted Father as the person of authority. It can be seen, therefore, that beyond the maternal relationship, as soon as I was conscious of anything, I was conscious of Father and then of our shipyard.

His was a commanding presence. My father stood six feet two inches in his stocking feet and weighed 215 pounds in his prime. At the age of seventy four (when I was ten), he had much of his black hair and could beat me in a foot race. High cheekbones characterized a rather narrow face, which was further accented by a prominent chin and a rather hawk-like nose. (He called it a "Roman nose.") The countenance, though often stern, still reflected an inner benevolence of spirit; he grinned easily. He wore his pince-nez glasses only for his extensive reading, and I don't recall that he had an extra ounce of fat on him. "People eat too much!" he used to say. Except for his final illness, I never knew him to be sick. As a younger man he was possessed of great physical strength, shipyard demonstrations of this being legendary. His thick, muscular hands were noticeable for the missing tip of the forefinger on the left one, a casualty of a hay chopper in his youth. In my recollection, his clothing seemed invariably to include one or more elements of a three-piece suit, made, one could be sure, by my tailor uncle. In winter he wore an overcoat only on Sundays or if he went out of town; in the shipyard he wore a heavy cardigan under the suitcoat and a pair of mittens. He was partial to detachable collars and bow ties, although he would wear a four-in-hand on occasion, never failing to tuck the ends into the front of his shirt. On his head was the traditional cloth visored cap with a button on top, or a broad-brimmed felt; the stump of an unlit cigar stuck from his mouth. Lastly, if it were a season of flowers, a small blossom plucked from Mother's garden, or perhaps a weed, would adorn the jacket buttonhole.

But it wasn't merely physical aspects that drew one's attention. It was the obvious rock-like integrity of character that he projected from within. His commanding presence was, I suspect, acquired in no small measure by a propensity for commanding—in family life and throughout his very active business life, and especially in the management of his shipyard.

In 1872, at the age of eighteen, Arthur Dana Story had gone into the shipbuilding business in partnership with Moses Adams, an older man, on the same ground where my great-grandfather, Abel Story, began in 1813. Arthur was the oldest of fourteen children. By the time I was born, April 10, 1919, he had launched 334 vessels and begat nine children of his own. He celebrated my arrival with the purchase of a magnificent tall clock, which today is one of my most cherished possessions. My mother, Ruby Adams, was his second wife, and I was her only child, born when she was forty-one. A difficult delivery was expected so she was taken to a private hospital on Newbury Street in Boston. Such was indeed the case. They almost lost us both. Praises be! The Lord and Dr. Webster triumphed, and I came home to spend my boyhood in a monstrous Victorian pile at 20 Winthrop Street in Essex.

Father wanted to name me Job after his father. "Nothing doing" said Mother. "No son of mine is going to be named Job." So they used Father's middle name instead. I think that name had come from author Richard Henry Dana. Another son, Arthur Dana Story, Jr., died at the age of eighteen.

As one of the town's more prosperous businessmen, Father was, as they used to say, in comfortable circumstances, although by no means did we dwell in the lap of luxury. Even had he been a really wealthy man he would never have condoned it. Frugality and conservatism were watchwords with him. We certainly had all we needed, and whatever we did buy was of the best quality. "You buy the best there is and that's poor enough," Father used to say.

With the visual acuity of hindsight, I think I can honestly say that the years of my boyhood in the mansard-roofed house at 20 Winthrop Street were the happiest of my life. The place was Victorian and so were my parents, but I didn't know that and wouldn't have cared if I had. Although the only child in the house, I was still part of a large family since my Uncle Lyndon Story lived next door and my half-brother and half-sisters and their families were mostly close by in Essex. Sister Georgia, for example, was just four houses down the street, next door to Aunt Julia. I sometimes wistfully expressed a desire for a small brother or sister, only to be answered with a smile or a pat on the head. Yet, even though at the time of my coming only four of us lived there (Mother had a live-in maid), a number of people seemed always to be in and about the house. Tradespeople of several sorts came nearly every day. Men came to confer with Father about his various business ventures; neighbors and relatives were forever stopping by, some for extended visits, and so it went.

Speaking of tradespeople—the word has a rather demeaning connotation, but I certainly don't use it in that sense—I remember Deacon Caleb Cogswell, who was our milk man. "Caley," we called him, was a deacon of our Congregational Church, the superintendent of the Sunday School, and one of the town's selectmen. I remember Phil Melanson, the iceman, who worked for Bert Mears; Clarence "Curly" Cook, the fishman who came at 6 A.M. with horse and wagon, blowing a little tin horn; T. Morris, the junk man (he took old newspapers, scrap metal, and unwanted hens); "Solly" Sundberg in his Wills Sainte Claire who brought around the Sunday papers; Mr. Lampropoulos, the banana man; Earl Eustace, the grain man who brought grain for the shipyard horse and who, to my delight, came in a 1915 Mack truck; two grocers, Lyman James and Grover Dodge; a lady from the church, Lottie Gardner Burnham, who came to collect the rent on pew sixty-five; Charlie Goodrich who came in his Pierce Arrow every couple of weeks peddling securities; and lastly, a Fuller Brush man whose name I don't recall; all these in addition to the chore boy each day.

"And chores," you say, "What were the chores a chore boy did?" Well, first of all he went down cellar for a hod of coal for the kitchen stove. Next, he took out the ashes from that stove and the big coal furnace, and then went down the street to fetch a fresh bucket of drinking water from the well in front of my Aunt Julia's, three houses away. Essex did not then have a public water system, and the water in our well smelled. When necessary he emptied the tub of meltwater from under the ice chest; he mowed the lawn and shovelled snow in season. Incidentally, the tub of meltwater was a nifty place for sailing toy boats. In common with many Essex houses, our water for domestic purposes came from a big brick cistern in the cellar, fed by run-off from the roof.

The job description of chore boy (or man) also included babysitting me when the occasion demanded. The last of the chore boys, and by far my favorite, was Sammy Gray, who came each morning to hitch up Jimmy, the shipyard horse, to the wagon and take him to the yard. It was Sammy and Jimmy who dragged the heavy timbers about the shipyard. Between times he painted and puttied. When the young fellows who had served as chore boys ultimately disappeared, Sammy assumed the job. He was a jovial and lusty little man, attired in denim jumper and rubber boots, whose noisy and cheerful arrival was a welcome event each morning. Along with the chores he always delivered an item or two of local news or gossip to keep things interesting. When doubling as a babysitter for me (and after my parents had disappeared), he would take me downtown or let me get up again if I had gone to bed.

Everyone in town knew Sammy. His shouts of greeting could be heard all over the neighborhood, and children and dogs came running. He had no family of his own. Curiously, many who had known him for years never realized that his proper name was George P. Gray. He was just "Sammy"; everyone knew who was meant.

Our house sat in a spacious yard with a splendid carriage barn in the back. There were lots of fruit trees, and the purple beech in the middle of the front lawn had to be the best climbing tree in town. In the days of Jimmy the horse, he was kept in that barn, which meant there was hay in the loft. Hay in the loft meant a superb place for kids to play, and with attractions like these, the kids of our neighborhood spent much of their time in our yard.

The existence of the shipyard seized my consciousness early on and, as soon as I was allowed away from home alone, I was drawn to climbing about the stagings and playing in and about the vessels. Days and days my friends and I would be there as soon as school let out. I quickly learned the nomenclature of a ship and its parts, and gained an appreciation of what the men were doing. Best of all, I got to know all the men and derived enormous pleasure in talking to them and watching them in their work. I watched Jack Doyle as he built the forecastles; I sat up in the shop as Ed Perkins got out the pieces for a skylight or a companionway and was with him as he built a cabin trunk; I was beside Stan Burnham as he cut in a hawse pipe or fitted a cabin portlight; I spent hours up in the timber field with my Uncle Eddie as he told me stories while molding timber; I teased old Liboire D'Entremont, the sawyer, until he agreed to saw out a toy boat for me. ("Lib" had a cleft palate and talked as though his mouth were full of mashed potato.) In utter fascination I watched Len Amero, Bill Atkins, and George Story (no relation) driving oakum into the seams and then Sammy or Bill Bagwell trowelling in the putty. I learned to stay clear of Walter Cox's planking gang; they wanted no

kids in the way on the stage—not when they were putting on
two streaks of plank a day. Little did I realize that one day he
would be working for me. Betimes "Mac" MacIver would
pause in dubbing frames and give me a nickel to run up to
Leighton Perkins's store for a fresh plug of chewing tobacco.
Ah, how it all filled me with wonder. The methods and processes by which a wooden ship was built were indelibly
etched upon my soul.

I speak of Jack Doyle. I have especially fond memories of
being in the forecastle as Jack worked. Working alone, he
would build maybe fourteen bunks with storage lockers in
front, a walk-in icebox, a coal bin, a shack locker (place for
ready grub), dish racks, a counter for the galley sink and
working area with lockers under, a hanging locker for oilskins,
a platform for the cook stove, the forecastle table, and stairs to
the deck—and do it all in less than three weeks. He had a tremendous capacity for work and for chewing tobacco. He built
the bulkhead between forecastle and fish hold, together with
the fixtures attached to it, last of all so that he could conven-
iently sweep his sawdust and shavings out into the bilge. As
the pile of dirt grew, the top of it was continually soaked with
tobacco juice. He came up out of the forecastle one day to spit
over the rail. The "splat" it made when it hit the stage was
thirty-two inches across. As I remember, Jack sometimes did
this work by the job, and it was obviously in his interest to get
it done quickly. He lived just across the street from the yard
and would be at work early in the morning and sometimes
long after the gang had gone home.

When Jack Doyle had completed his carpenter work, John
Closson came in to finish it out—to varnish and paint. John,
as I remember, was a man of rather ample dimensions who
worked as an independent contractor and whose rather forbid-
ding mien precluded the presence of spectators the likes of me.
The underside of the deck and the deckbeams were painted
white, while all the other work, bunks, lockers, cabinets, etc.,
were varnished bright. I only saw John when he came to the
house to get his checks.

A completed forecastle was one of the slickest places for

kids to play that one can imagine. It was one thing for us kids to be playing in the forecastles of the fishermen, but it was something else again when it came to yachts. In 1926 Father built the *Faith*, a beautiful ketch-rigged yacht for a Mr. Walden W. Shaw of Chicago. She was big, too: 147 gross tons. Magnificently appointed, she had a large main saloon amidships reached by a grand staircase from the main deck—all constructed by Ed Perkins. Mr. Shaw chanced to come on deck one day to discover a bunch of us kids running up and down this staircase. A few well-chosen words from him put a stop to that and to any more frolicking about on that vessel. It was the same Mr. Shaw, by the way, who discovered that our yard had no surface planer and accordingly made Father a present of one. It was the same planer that came with the yard when, years later, I bought the place.

Lib D'Entremont was another with a prodigious capacity for hard work. As the sawyer working with oak timbers and plank, the work was heavy enough anyway, but Lib had a rather cranky disposition and preferred to work mostly alone. Only Sammy could get along with him. He pushed literally tens of thousands of board feet of oak and hard pine through that old band saw, wearing out two saw tables in the process. He once worked for two days with a broken arm without realizing it. He, too, lived next to the yard and would come down early in the morning to file his saws and stay late to saw up scrap firewood. To facilitate the saw-filing, he used a pair of somebody else's cast-off spectacles.

"Lib, please saw me out a boat?"

"Get away from here, kid. I ain't got time for that now!"

"Please, Lib?"

"Oh, all right. Give it here and I'll saw it. Now, get out of here!"

I developed a sort of special friendship with Frank White Story (no relation). Known simply as "Frank White," he was a fastener, whose job it was to bore holes for bolts and trunnels and then drive them in. It was great fun to watch the long augurs sink down into the keelson, maybe, or see the chips come curling out of a trunnel hole. He seemed to enjoy my company and always maintained a smiling and friendly demeanor towards me. I never knew until long afterwards that he had a severely retarded child at home who was kept in a crib in the kitchen.

I regret that there was one man whom we kids sort of picked on. He was Tom Irving, a bent old man who came to work every day on the bus from Gloucester. He usually had on a battered old felt hat and wore a bandana around his neck. In his earlier years he had been a shipbuilder himself, with a little yard of his own situated on a Gloucester wharf. In launching vessels he literally tipped them up and slid them over the edge. At various times he subcontracted to build hulls for Father. We, of course, didn't know any of this, and wouldn't have cared anyway, as we searched him out to drop chips on his head or holler at him. He finally complained to Father and that put a stop to that.

I must say something about "Pete and Skeet," the outboard joiners. An inboard joiner performed the finish work in cabins and forecastles; an outboard joiner smoothed up the outside of the hulls. Pete (Peter Hubbard) and Skeet (John Doyle) were the outboard joiners in our yard. They worked together as a team for years. Using smoothing planes, they first "traversed" the seams between the planks—meaning that the plane was used across the seam—and then with jack planes and fore planes, they planed the seams and planks the long way. Finally, using flat metal scrapers, the ultimate finished surface was achieved. This, generally speaking, was like glass. Imagine covering the hull of a 125-foot vessel in this way! Nobody ever heard of power sanders.

Edwin James Story was one of Father's younger brothers. To me he was Uncle Eddie; to every else he was Eddie James. To him I was "Day," the only nickname I ever had. Uncle Eddie and I hit it off well. In the shipyard his principal task was molding timber, meaning that he took the molds or patterns of the various timbers and, after selecting appropriate pieces, would trace out the shapes with a race knife. His shipyard work was not where his heart really lay. He was an artist—a musician—who marched to a different drum. Music was indeed his first love. He had great talent and played oboe, English horn, clarinet, and saxophone. For many years he played in theater orchestras in Boston and once travelled for several seasons with Barnum and Bailey's circus band. Some of his escapades on these tours branded him as something of a black sheep with the rest of the family. Father once referred to him as a "damn fiddler." Curiously, he had served for a time as the town's truant officer, pursuing his culprits on his bicycle. (The kids called him Peter Piper.)

Most people in town thought of Eddie James as the town photographer. He began in 1900 taking photos of the shipyards and scenes about the town. He built a splendid little studio and darkroom on Western Avenue near his house, and it was to this studio that Essex folks repaired to have their pictures taken. There was a dais with a piano bench on it and a woodland scene behind. Here the clients sat (including my parents and me) while Uncle Eddie removed a lens cap, counted to three, and then clapped the cap back on.

With his travels and multifarious experiences, Uncle Eddie was possessed of a fund of stories that, much to my delight, he would relate to me as he rolled over the timbers and I sat on a nearby log. He would instruct me in deep breathing exercises, and we enjoyed whistling a duet of "The Whistler and his Dog." Recalling the words of St. Paul in 1 Corinthians, chapter 15, verse 52 (words commonly used in the burial of the dead), he once queried me, "Day, do you suppose that when the last trumpet sounds, all those folks up there in the old cemetery will rise up and peek over the wall to see what's going on down here in the shipyard?"

As might be imagined, this sort of thing sometimes consumed Uncle Eddie's attention to the point that the supply of timbers to the sawmill began to diminish, much to Father's irritation. He once came up to the hillside where Uncle Eddie was working with the rebuke, "Eddie—ye have compassed this mountain long enough!"

To digress a bit, let me speak about the shipyard itself. Our yard was a plot of perhaps two acres or more, bordering the upper bend of the Essex River right next to the bridge and in the very center of town. The shipways extended in from Main Street to a point where the river curved away. As many as nine vessels have been set up in this distance. The vessels themselves would generally measure from 60 feet to as much as 175 feet in length and maybe 15 to 30 feet wide. Towards the back, the land extended to the next street and up the hill for a bit. This area was given over to the storage of the oak timber and planking from which the vessels were constructed. In my day, a two-story building, 28 by 38 feet, stood towards the front of the yard. This housed the joiner shop and the table saw upstairs, with tool chest and heavy equipment storage downstairs. Also downstairs was a room for the paint locker and another room containing a pot-bellied stove, which was referred to as "the office." Actually, it was not really the yard office, but just a handy warm gathering place for the gang to play high-low-jack on rainy days. Arranged under the stairs were the barrels of bungs and trunnel wedges, while in the cellar were kegs and kegs of ship spikes and clinch rings. The real office was Father's big roll-top desk in the front parlor at home where the telephone was, with an extension in the kitchen; in his day there was never a telephone at the yard or electric lights in the shop.

Standing in the midst of the yard was a smallish building housing such power machinery as we had: a thirty-eight-inch band saw, a trunnel lathe, and a large grindstone—all driven by leather belts and powered by one large electric motor. A boiler, which had once powered the band saw but now supplied steam to the steaming box, was in there, too. This was strictly the domain of Lib D'Entremont. By my time, the boring of holes was done with portable electric drills, but no other portable power tools or machines were used. One can easily deduce from this that, in our yard (and, in fact, in all Essex yards), most things were done by hand.

Two other small structures in the yard completed the picture. One was a little shed at the very back of the yard where the highly flammable oakum (Tarred hemp fibers) and cotton for caulking the seams were kept and which was used by the caulkers as a place to "spin" oakum. That's the process by which the strand of oakum is drawn out from the tight bales, stretched, and rolled over one knee in preparation for driving. The caulkers did this at various odd times and on rainy days. The other little building stood down by the creek and was (you guessed it) the yard toilet. This affair was hardly more than a shelter over a wood railing. In those days we didn't have environmentalists; in fact, they used to say that the best eels were speared in that creek.

From the time of my birth in April of 1919 until he died in March 1932, my father and his men completed ninety more vessels, with a total gross tonnage of 9,408, or an average of 104.5 per boat. In two of those years there were ten; in three there were nine. These ships included seven three-masted coasting schooners, most of which were about 160 feet on deck; three contenders for the International Fisherman's Trophy—the schooners *Henry Ford*, *Columbia*, and *Gertrude L. Thebaud*; five lovely schooner or ketch yachts; one patrol boat for the Commonwealth of Massachusetts; one patrol boat for the U.S. Customs Service; one tug; and seventy-two schooners, trawlers, and draggers for the Gloucester and Boston fishing fleets. Many of these were big ones.

Throughout those years the shipyard gang (shipyard crews were universally referred to as "gangs") numbered only thirty to thirty-five men. Though, as we have mentioned, practically everything was done by hand, and though they worked out-of-doors the year round, theirs was a remarkable productivity. They were good at what they did. With a six-day work week (no coffee breaks), they turned out an average Gloucesterman in about ninety days. The big racing schooner *Columbia* was 140 feet on deck. When she launched on April 17, 1923, she had been completed in 102 working days by a gang numbering exactly thirty men, working through one of the worst winters on record. Moreover, during that same period, another smaller schooner had been completed, and a third was started and partly framed out.

For a young and very impressionable boy, those were heady and exciting times. I never thought of my father as being old, though he was. He loved kids, and it never bothered him to have them around. My friends and I were in and about the shipyard much of the time. He took me with him on his business errands whenever possible, and many is the time he invited a bunch of us to ride with him in the old Buick. We often took turns sitting in his lap and steering the car. Imagine! Still and all, he left no doubt in my mind that he meant what he said. I learned to do as I was told. To him I was always "Boy," and if he said, "Come, Boy, come!" I came. Fortunately for me, if I needed a whipping or a spanking, he usually contrived to have Mother do it.

It's a good thing that neither of them saw what I did one day when I was cavorting with some of my playmates downtown near the shipyard. From behind a parked car, I darted into the street directly in the path of two gentlemen bearing down on me in a large Pierce Arrow roadster. They stopped about three feet in front of me and eloquently upbraided this stupid kid for doing such a thing. Perhaps it's well that I encountered Pierce Arrow brakes instead of those on a Model T.

In all probability, my friends and I had been playing in Charlie Hanson's spar yard. (His proper name was Charles Hanson Andrews.) The yard was across the street from our shipyard and in behind Lyman James's boat sheds. It was Charlie and his men—Harry Story, Scott Lambert, Joe Tibbets, and Art Gates—who made all the masts and other spars for the James yard and our own. They also made derricks and flagpoles. This, too, was a grand place for us to play (after the men had gone home). There were always long spars in various stages of completion set up on trestles upon which we could climb and run. In addition, there was generally a large group of raw sticks rafted up in the little salt creek next to the yard, upon which it was even more fun to leap about and perhaps fall overboard. We discovered that a mast has some remarkable acoustical properties. In fascination one of us would put an ear to one end while another scratched ever so lightly on the other end. The sound was perfectly transmitted the length of the mast. For a number of years Charlie was my Sunday school teacher. I don't recall that we ever got a great deal of instruction in the Bible, but we sure heard a lot of wonderful stories about the spars he had made, whom he made them for, and where they went. He loved people and loved to talk about them.

It was Father's custom to go to the bank in Gloucester every Saturday morning to get the cash for the payroll. Because it was Saturday—no school—I would almost always go with him. Going first to the bank, he would stuff the large bundle of bills into his inside coat pocket and proceed from there to do the rest of his business. Once, when I was still quite a little chap, we called at the office of an old lawyer acquaintance who observed as we entered, "My, young man, aren't you having a good time with Grandpa this morning."

"Oh," said I, "that ain't my grandpa, that's my father!"

With a hearty laugh and a slap on the back he exclaimed, "Why, Arthur, I didn't know!"

He was Arthur to most people and to the gang in the yard. He was also commonly referred to simply as "A.D." or among the townsfolk as "Arthur Daney." (In Essex the custom of the vernacular often converted names ending in "a" to "ey.") This distinguished him from the host of other Storys who dwelt in Essex. If someone were looking for a job, or to sell him something, or to borrow some money, he was "Mr. Story." To Mother and me, and to all of the family, he was "Pa."

Another of his frequent Gloucester errands was to look in at the blacksmith shop where the ironwork for the hull and spars was made. It had long been the custom for an Essex shipbuilder to supply three things: the hull with all joiner and finish work; the spars (masts, booms, gaffs, and clubs); and the ironwork necessary to rig the vessel. The ironwork consisted of chainplates, stem irons for bobstays, gammon irons, sheet horses, and miscellaneous heavy eyebolts; on the spars, it was all of the numerous bands and eyes to which the rigging was attached. In earlier years, all of these items were made by Essex shipsmiths, the last of whom, Otis Story, gave up in the middle 1920s. After that, the shops in Gloucester supplied the ironwork, and it was to these that I would accompany Father. It was with some apprehension that I went into a shop— dark and sooty as it was with sparks, red-hot iron, the roar of a blower, and the clanging of hammers on anvils. The atmosphere was heavy with the pervasive smell of soft--coal smoke.

The man whose shop I remember best was Charlie Thistle, a great bear of a figure, whose totally bald head glistened like a crystal ball. Though his shop was in Gloucester, Charlie lived in Essex. I stood before the counter in Leighton Perkins's general store one afternoon, trying to decide what I could get Mother for Mother's Day, when Charlie came in and, seeing me, inquired what I was doing. When I told him, he said, "Oh, look, what you want are some flowers, not something from a hardware store. You come with me and we'll get something nice for her." He took me to Gordon's Greenhouse in nearby Ipswich and helped me pick out a bouquet. Of course it turned out that I didn't have nearly enough allowance money to pay for it. Never mind. Charlie graciously made up the difference.

One other ancillary trade existed in my time, and that was the windlass maker. All Essex fishing schooners carried a heavy large-barrelled wooden anchor windlass that was made in a local shop. Most of ours were made by Albert Noah ("Bert Noah") Story, assisted by his sons Len and Harry in their shop at Essex Falls. Their modus operandi was straight out of the fifteenth century. If the *Santa Maria* had a windlass, and I presume she did, it couldn't have been made any differently from the way they made theirs. There was one other shop that I recall, and that was Archer Poland's over in South Essex. (He also did the lofting, but more of that later.) Archie used tools and equipment somewhat more modern. In the early years of Essex shipbuilding there were still other shops that made wooden pumps, wooden tackle blocks, and anchor stocks.

Throughout my boyhood the routine of daily living was fairly predictable. On weekdays Father arose without fail at six o'clock. (On Sundays it was seven.) Once up, he expected anybody else in the house to be up as well. After dressing and putting on his barn slippers, his first order of business was to go to the barn to feed Jimmy, the shipyard horse, and clean out his stall. Finished with this, he came in and sat down in his Morris chair for a bit while he read aloud from his Bible, after which he would go to the yard to get the gang started and have a look at whatever would be taking place during the forenoon. Starting time at the yard was 7 A.M. About 7:15 he came back to the house to have breakfast, shave in the kitchen with a straight razor, and perhaps do a little desk work or make a phone call.

More than likely breakfast included some hearty leftovers from the day before: chowder, beans, hash, pie. This was a substantial meal. I always came home from school to eat since we had an hour at noon and the school was hardly more than 150 yards down the street. Father regularly followed his dinner with a thirty-minute snooze on the living room couch, after which it was back to the yard or attendance upon some of his other business interests. These, it must be mentioned, included ownership of nine houses besides the one we lived in, a 165-acre farm with more than twenty cows, a three-masted coasting schooner, a good-sized yacht yard in Gloucester, a miniature golf course (which he wouldn't dream of trying), the local picnic grove (which we did try), and the A&P store. For good measure, he was a partner in a wholesale fish business in Boston, a director of two banks, a trustee of the public library, and a member of his church's governing parish committee. One could really stretch things, I suppose, and include part ownership of several Gloucester fishing vessels whose shares, notes, or mortgages he held in lieu of payment. In earlier years he had twice served in the Massachusetts House of Representatives, had been a candidate for state senator, and had been a member of the electoral college that cast its votes for William McKinley.

Following our six o'clock supper, the evenings were spent in reading or more desk work. Occasionally my parents got together with friends for an evening of auction bridge. Father took it upon himself to put me to bed until I was old enough to do it myself. By that time I was old enough to go with Father and/or Mother to a Monday or Thursday evening movie show in the hall over the post office.

Father had a personal idiosyncrasy that was comical, interesting, or disgusting, depending on the sensibilities of the observer. We had a privy in the backyard. (Back then, I guess, every house in town had one, either freestanding or tucked away in a barn or woodshed.) It was quite an elegant one, built in the style of the house, and was connected to the house by a high board fence. Old-timer that he was, Father preferred it to the bathroom in the house and would sit in there with the door wide open—the better to enjoy the view, I suppose, or to observe whatever was going on in his yard, which was frequently full of kids and their games, or serving as a convenient short-cut for the people who lived on Maple Street behind the barn. The kids giggled and the ladies passing through averted their eyes. My mother was forced to contain her dismay.

In the shipyard Father frequently positioned himself on a plank or sawhorse under a tree in the middle of the yard where he could watch what was going on. Occasionally he roamed about, taking a closer look and making a few well-chosen remarks here or there. He was noted as a man of few words, not given to talk for talk's sake. When he did speak, it was short and to the point. He had worked as a ship carpenter in his earlier years, and he was thoroughly acquainted with how things ought to be and how a job should be done. Curiously, in my time, I can't recall ever seeing him so much as drive a nail.

The men learned early on that a simple suggestion meant they'd better hop to it. He used to say, "One of these days I want you to do such and such." The man addressed knew that "one of these days" meant now! With impatience he would sometimes exclaim, "Come on, come; get a move on!" Though generally tolerant of human frailties, Father could get royally mad on occasion. Once he assigned Dave Languedoc to start getting out a stem. Dave put the mold on a piece and lined it out. When he cut it, however, he cut it to the rabbet line instead of the profile. Father gave him a chewing out and then fired him. The firing didn't last too long for in a short while Dave was back at work. He could be gruff and abrupt and would brook no nonsense, but A.D. had a soft heart and demonstrated in many ways his concern for his men. In slack times he would start a vessel on speculation to keep the gang together; he could be counted on for a quick touch to tide a man over an emergency, or even a more substantial loan (at no interest) for an expense deemed necessary. He visited his men when they were sick, and if there was nobody else to do it, he buried them when they died. He tried to be fair. In return he received the loyalty of most, and yes, the affection of many.

I have been speaking about a number of men of our ship-yard gang and of a few others. Though I haven't mentioned them all, by any means, I knew them all and I can quite honestly say I liked them all. I have no recollection of anyone who was not friendly to me. A great many were colorful characters, men not afraid to be unique or simply to be unapologetically themselves.

A majority of our ship carpenters were family men maintaining a home and bringing up children on fifty to sixty cents an hour. Many men did this and sent kids off to school on less than $1,000 cash income per year. They helped themselves along in a number of ways: they had gardens; they raised hens; some kept a cow; they went clamming and fishing; a few had a part-time job on the side. Bill Swett, one of our men, was the Essex police chief; Sammy Gray worked in Leighton Perkins's general store. For fuel they burned shipyard scrap wood bought for $2 a wagon-load. In the area of schooling, hardly a man had more than an elementary education. Some who came over from Nova Scotia didn't even have that.

There was an element of loyalty to the yard where they worked. It was not common for a man to shift yards. Each thought of himself, and was regarded by others, as a Story man or a James man. The caulkers sometimes moved about, following their trade, but rarely did a carpenter do this. I suppose this could romantically be thought of as an esprit de corps, but I'm sure the men didn't consciously regard it as such. They were not given to sentimentality or emotionalism. They had no awareness of their socio-economic status; one would have had difficulty explaining to them what that meant. Within the context of their time and place, they had reasonably good jobs. They were interested in making a living building good vessels and were proud of what they could do.

I would be less than candid if I did not mention the predilec-
tion for alcohol among many of the shipyard men. As I think
back it seems they were mostly either teetotalers or rummies.
Oh, I suppose there were a few who used alcohol in modera-
tion, but generally it was those who drank and those who
didn't. Happily, those who didn't were in the great majority.
Have in mind that in the early years of the nineteenth century
it was common practice in the shipyards to break twice a day
to allow each man his ration of rum.

The ones who drank really went at it. Essex was always a
"dry" town in the years before Prohibition, so booze had to be
bought from a number of local entrepreneurs who sold it sur-
repticiously, or one went to Gloucester on the electric cars on
Saturday nights. Here they patronized the "rum shops" down
Duncan Street, using up a good part of a week's pay envelope
and needing assistance to board a car for home. Some of them
used to go on bats and would be drunk for a week at a time. I
must say that the work these men performed in the shipyard
was good work or they wouldn't have been there. I had some
experience with men in this category, which will be mentioned
as we go along. An expression of the vernacular that cropped
up for years was the parting remark of one man to another,
"I'll meet ya on the last car!"

In the early years of Essex shipbuilding, which, by the way,
went back to the 1650s, boats were built, sparred and rigged,
and sailed out of the Essex River. In the later years, at the time
of launching, a tug would be waiting to take the new vessel to
Gloucester or Boston for the stepping of the spars and the installation of engines and machinery. For these the owners
were responsible. This system certainly simplified matters as
far as Essex shipyards were concerned. We could concentrate
on the actual construction at which we excelled. There was no
need for cranes, outfitting wharves, and shops with all of their
attendant equipment and personnel. Gloucester was well
geared to that sort of thing.

Times of launching were splendid occasions, especially for a
kid. In our own yard, from 1919 until 1932, they occurred anywhere from four to ten times a year; add to that the launchings

from the James yard, also very active in that period, and one can appreciate the extent of this activity. Two sons of the ould sod, Jack Murphy or Jack Doyle, supervised the preparation of the launchways. For an unusually large or heavy vessel, or one likely to attract a crowd, the standard upright launching in a cradle was the method used. In Essex, however, and also in Gloucester, a technique known as a "side launching" was generally employed. This doesn't mean that the vessel entered the water sideways; it was instead a process in which the vessel was first leaned over onto a single sliding ways built up under one bilge, and then the keel was brought to bear on a series of greased slabs laid crosswise to it. This method effected a far greater economy of stock and labor than the traditional one, and there were far fewer pieces of lumber to fish out of the water afterwards. Moreover, it sent the vessel into the water nearly on her beam ends where the water was shallow.

While somewhat more risky, a side launching was much more spectacular than an upright one. In fact, if the observer understood what was happening, it could be quite exciting. The procedure that brought the weight of the boat to bear on the slabs was the interesting part. With the ways on only one side, it meant that the other side presented a space free and clear for the men to work. They began at the after end of the vessel. Working forward they split out the wooden blocks on which the vessel had been sitting during construction, at the same time driving long slim wedges under the aforementioned slabs. This, you see, gradually transferred the weight of the vessel from the blocks to the greased slabs. The fun came in not knowing how many blocks would be split out before she started to move. My friends and I would sit on the ancient mound of chips beside the ways and stare expectantly as the men progressed.

As the bow of the vessel was approached, we would notice that she was beginning to creep a little and suddenly the splitting of the next block would set her free. Away she would go in a cloud of smoking grease and, with a mighty splash and creaking of the ways, plunge into the river. Three long blasts on the steam whistle of the waiting tug completed the picture.

Wow! It was even more fun to launch aboard the vessel.

The launching part wasn't all there was to it, however. At once, with the vessel overboard, attention was directed to the "drag." This was the device by which the momentum of the vessel, once afloat, was arrested and hopefully stopped. The drag was a bundle of oak timbers bound around with a heavy chain and fastened to the vessel by a long and heavy hawser coiled on the ground near the bow. If things had been figured out right, the hawser would come taut as soon as the vessel was fully afloat, and the drag would leap into motion and slide over the ground toward the ways. All of this was necessary because of the narrowness of the river. It was exciting to see that big bundle of timber suddenly jerked into action. If too much slack had been left in the hawser, the drag, of course, never moved, and the vessel stuck her rudder into the mud of the marsh island opposite the yard. If perchance the drag, once in motion, fetched up against something solid, the hawser would part with a mighty "twang" and the ends go whistling through the air. Again the vessel would plow into the marsh island. Builders, Father included, very often made up a drag using the keel timbers of the next vessel to occupy that berth, thereby killing two birds with one stone.

My mother—in some ways a timid soul—steadfastly refused to attend launchings because she didn't want to be there if something untoward happened. She didn't like thunderstorms and she didn't care for boats or the water. She had been present at the launching of the big three-master *Nat L. Gorton* in July of 1916 when the launching cradle collapsed and the vessel fell over. She vowed never to attend another launching. She was, however, greatly concerned that things go well and so worked out a dandy little arrangement with her friend Alice Porter (Burnham) whose house was just across the creek from the shipyard and who would telephone her immediately when the boat was in the water. I can remember the occasions when I was sick and couldn't be in the shipyard (or in school, either) at launching time. I would hear the tug's whistle and at once the phone would ring. It would be Alice Porter.

As one can well imagine, the launching of vessels weighing anywhere from 50, say, to perhaps 300, 400, or even 500 tons was fraught with the possibility of error or mishap. The *Nat L. Gorton*, just referred to, probably weighed close to 300 tons and was accordingly placed in a cradle. At launching time, one sliding way was severed before the other—instead of at the same instant as was supposed to happen. The cradle wracked and the shores fell out. Over she went. Father hired a crew of building movers to come and right her up.

The lovely schooner *Columbia* rammed the marsh island and, because the proper braces had not been put on the rudder, the rudder post was sprung. The seiner *St. Rita* plunged off the end of her ways, and the after end of the keel stuck in the mud of the river bottom. The tide went out and there she was—half ashore and half in the riverbed. The schooner *Radio* was launched and, through a quirk of design, rolled down to starboard and stayed there. Somebody left an open gallon of black paint on the deck of the *Louis A. Thebaud*. When she went, so did the black paint—all over a pearl gray deck. When the moment of launching theoretically arrived, many vessels just stuck there, refusing to budge. If jacks and/or a line from the towboat didn't bring results, the ways would have to be taken apart and regreased. This was expensive.

What might have been a tragic accident was narrowly averted in the launching of the *Joseph and Lucia*. The vessel was given a traditional Essex side launching, but the slope of the ways was less than the slope of the keel so that, as the vessel slid down, she righted up and fell over on the side away from the ways. Fortunately she was sufficiently into the water that it absorbed her fall and she righted up again—not, however, before striking the forefoot on a large rock. I had a couple of episodes of my own, which we'll describe in due course.

A couple of launchings in particular stand out in my memory. The first was the launching of Father's three-masted schooner *Adams*, named for Mother, on the thirteenth of April 1929. She was a big vessel, 370 gross tons and about 160 feet on deck. What made the launching so special was the fact that she had been sitting there right next to Main Street since the

late summer of 1920. Her long pole bowsprit projected right
out over the street. As might be imagined, she had become
something of a landmark, a sight people looked for as they
rode through Essex.

Father had built her to his own account in the flush of pros-
perity right after World War I. Almost as soon as she was
framed out, the bloom was off the economic rose, so to speak,
and he stopped the work. He had muffed an opportunity to
sell her, feeling, I think, that if he held off a bit he would get a
better price. Instead, he was stuck with her. From time to
time, as opportunity arose, he would resume the work, until
by the spring of 1923 she was virtually complete. The trouble
was that by then nobody wanted a three-masted schooner, so
she just sat there.

At some point during those years she became home to a
swarm of bees. When the chainplates were put on, one of the
fastening bolts had been left out, leaving a hole into the space
between plank and ceiling. The bees found this hole and in
they went. They were there right up until the time of launching. It seemed a shame to waste all of the honey that must
have been in there. At various times feature writers for a number of local papers heard about this and did pieces on it. Without exception, they would conclude that this occurrence pres-
aged good luck for the vessel. It didn't.

In the winter of 1918-1919 Father had built the sister ship to
the *Adams*. Named *Lincoln*, she had been successfully engaged
in the coasting trade between the Canadian Maritimes, Boston,
and New York when, on the night of September 10, 1928, off
Chatham, Cape Cod, she was rammed by the Boston collier *Se-
wall's Point* and broken nearly in two. Because she was loaded
with lumber she was in effect a solid block of wood and did
not sink. The Coast Guard cutter *Active* took her in tow and
brought her to Gloucester where the cargo was discharged.

At this point Father decided to use the *Adams* as a replacement and so, once again, the gang was put aboard to finish her
up. By now, after all this time in the sun and rain, her deck
was pretty spongy and most of it, including many deck beams,
had to be replaced. She also needed a complete recaulking.

Anyway, by April she was ready. As word of her impending launch got around, interest in the event grew by leaps and bounds. My poor mother, out there in her kitchen, handled ninety-nine inquiring phone calls.

Saturday, April 13, 1929, the day of the launching, brought an enormous crowd to Essex. It also brought an easterly snowstorm driving the spring tide even higher. The tug couldn't come over the outer bar into the river because of the seas, but the die was cast and the *Adams* had to go. Because of her size she was launched in a cradle. Father never even bothered to have her christened. The launching went all right, but they had to tie her off in the river basin using trees for bitts. As he supervised this operation, Father, who was then seventy-four years old, was wading around in water up to his knees. The *Adams*, as it turned out, was the last wooden three-masted commercial vessel to be launched in the U.S.A.

The other launching that I particularly remember was that of the lovely contender for the International Fisherman's Trophy, the schooner *Gertude L. Thebaud*, on March 17, 1930. The time for building a creation of this sort had long since passed, but Captain Ben Pine was not one to give up easily. Who could know? He might yet conquer his old adversary Angus Walters and his *Bluenose*. Besides, he had an angel in the person of one Louis Thebaud who would pay most of the bill. (The vessel was named for Mrs. Thebaud.)

She was built in the winter of 1929-30 and was ready by March. The enormous publicity surrounding the international schooner races of the early 1920s served to generate yet more for the *Thebaud*. Media hype was evident back then, except that in those days it was the news reels and radio as well as the newspapers. Published reports of her scheduled launching attracted a tremendous crowd when the day came. With a socialite group of sponsors, a large number of dignitaries and beautiful people were in attendance. The christening was handled by Miss Elizabeth Hovey, a pretty young debutante from Boston and a very competent sailor in her own right. In honor of this great occasion the public schools of Essex were dismissed to allow all the children to witness the event.

Amid a cacophony of cheers, tugboat whistles, and auto horns, the launching went off splendidly. However, whether it was Jack Murphy or Jack Doyle who got her ready, I'll never know because I wasn't there. Where was I? Wandering around the schoolyard wondering where everybody was. For reasons that I also will never know, I didn't get word of what was up. I think I must have run home for lunch only to return and find the place empty. I missed the whole show!

On the subject of launchings, I must mention that concomitant with these occasions was the happy custom among Essex folks of "going around in her." This meant that, in seasons of clement weather, the tug would take the new vessel alongside and warp her in to one side of the two small wharves in the upper river. Here, anyone who wanted to could clamber aboard and enjoy a lovely ride down the river, across Ipswich Bay, through the Annisquam River, and thence into Gloucester Harbor. Sometimes on warm summer days the tug would take the vessel all the way out around Cape Ann. Whole families, complete with picnic hampers, would enjoy this absolutely delightful excursion. Upon arrival in Gloucester, the trip back home was made by trolley car or, in my time, by bus. In earlier years, people walked the seven miles back to Essex.

I have alluded earlier to the 1919 Buick, the first car my parents owned. Until purchasing that car, Father's transportation had been a horse and buggy. The Buick was a club coupe and was supposed to be my mother's car. It was nice for her because it had a hand throttle in the middle of the steering wheel, and a cousin had taught her to drive using the hand throttle. I guess Father must have taught himself to drive. He used the foot throttle, but the trouble was, he never lifted his foot off the accelerator as he shifted gears, nor did he bother using second speed. By 1927 they both seemed to feel it was time for another car—something a little better, maybe. The Buick was looking pretty shabby, and Father was using it so much that Mother thought it was time for him to get a car of his own. Accordingly, Father swapped the old Buick for a secondhand later model, and one day in May took Mother over to the Packard place in Newburyport where Whitey Hayes sold them a lovely new tan and beige club coupe. (In 1928 Father traded the lemon he had bought for a spanking new Ford Model A.)

Mother was very proud of her new car. It also had a hand throttle in the middle of the steering wheel that worked the way the old one did. She and Father began to take occasional short trips in it chauffeured by grandson Don Goodhue or caulker George Story from the yard. Needless to say, I was delighted with this magnificent conveyance. Since his own Model A was only a two-passenger coupe, Father continued to borrow Mother's car from time to time if it was necessary to take along more than one other. One day Mother had just finished shining up the Packard and washing its windows when Father showed up and took it to lug some of the gang to Gloucester to finish up a job. Now it was his habit to chew a little Prince Albert tobacco, crimp cut, which he carried in his vest or the watch pocket of his pants. In due course, as he rode along, he turned to let fly out the window, except that the window was closed. The glass was so clean he couldn't see it! The gang never forgot—and neither did Mother.

I don't believe I could have been much over nine or ten when I, myself, learned to drive. I have mentioned how Father would let us kids sit in his lap and steer the old Buick; that, indeed, was my introduction to driving. Often I was with him when he went to look in on the operations of his farm, and he would drive out into the midst of a big field and let me steer the old girl where I would. One day he announced to me that now I should do the driving. From observation I pretty well knew how to operate the controls, albeit I could scarcely reach the pedals. So with him beside me I tried it out and, saints be praised, there I was—driving! Away we went, around and around in that field, Father with a grin from ear to ear. At length I graduated from the field to the roadway leading to the barnyard and got so I would take her way up the road, turn around and come back again—alone, too. I did this one day and came around the bend into the yard with undue haste, somehow managing to bring her to a stop about six inches from the barn door. All of this didn't seem to bother Father. It wasn't long after this that my nephew, the same Don Goodhue (nine years older than I was), had me driving his father's Model T pickup truck around the depot yard downtown.

I have mentioned Father's custom of going to Gloucester for the payroll every Saturday morning. Upon his arrival back home it then became Mother's job to take the cash and make up the payroll, putting the appropriate amount of money in each man's envelope. She did this every Saturday from the time they were married until Father died. Sick or well, she performed that task. I remember hearing her remark once that she could be lying there dying, but if it was a Saturday, she'd have to get up and do the payroll.

She worked at Father's big roll-top desk, stacking the envelopes in front of her. When she finished, she put them in a small brown leather satchel with fringe all around it, and Father took the satchel and me down to the yard where it pleased me to run around with it distributing the envelopes. Obviously, Saturday was a full workday. Furthermore, since the work was performed out of doors the year round, the weather was an important factor in whether or not a man got a full week's pay, although I must say conditions had to be fairly severe before a man would quit.

In those days, outdoor men were not the sun worshippers we see so much of today. Summer or winter they were always well clad. In the hottest days of summer it wasn't at all uncommon to see men—especially the older ones—with the sleeves of long underwear showing. The common bib-type overalls were standard among the men of the yard, with either a denim jumper or a worn suitcoat as outerwear. Many of the men wore old dress shirts, and not a few included a necktie. One could tell an inboard joiner by his khaki pants and carpenter's apron, which carried the advertisement of a local building supply house.

When I was ten, Father decided that I should go to summer camp. Suddenly, at a stroke, my little idyllic world from Winthrop Street to the shipyard was to be rudely shattered. From a vantage point of 60 years later, I can fully appreciate that the experience was indeed good for me and just what I needed. I did not, however, think so at the time. Resistance to the idea was futile. Father had decided and that's all there was to it. Accordingly, on July 3, 1929, after a train trip from Boston (I liked that), I arrived at Camp Ossipee on the shores of Lake Ossipee, New Hampshire. Here I was in what to me was an alien world populated by eighty or ninety lusty, enthusiastic adolescents from ten to sixteen years old—all of whom, I swear, were delighted to be there. At home, most of the playmates of my neighborhood were girls, and now to find myself in any such milieu as this was a little unsettling. Coming from New York and New Jersey, as many of these chaps did, they didn't even sound like me. We, of course, lived in tents and responded to bugle calls for everything we did from reveille to taps. I was not then, nor am I now, athletically inclined, but never mind. I did the whole bit, sports and all, though not, perhaps, with the vigor of my mates. The nature walks weren't too bad; I liked working with leather in the crafts shop; I used up Kodak film like there was no tomorrow; but, damn it all, they made me learn to swim!

My dear mother, who appreciated how much of her own make-up I possessed, did her best to placate me and wrote faithfully twice a week with all the news of home. From time to time she sent along some goodies and a couple of nifty mechanical toy boats, one of which I sank the first time I tried it. She and Father drove up to see me a number of times, and it was on one of these visits that there came another of his tobacco juice episodes. The owner and director of Camp Ossipee was Mr. John Calvin Bucher, a veritable paradigm of refined and scholarly dignity, complete with knickers and a Vandyke beard. Mr. Bucher was the headmaster of the Peekskill Military Academy in Peekskill, New York. My parents were standing in pleasant conversation with Mr. Bucher when Father suddenly turned aside and spit. Well, honest! Poor Mother could have sunk into the ground in embarrassment. As soon as they were out of earshot, she came down on him like a ton of bricks. I really think the incident continued to embarrass her for the rest of her life, if her retelling of it was any indication.

Though not connected with Camp Ossipee, there was another incident from which my mother never recovered. My sister Georgia's husband was Wilfred W. "Tony" Lufkin, a former congressman from our district, and later the Collector of Customs for the Port of Boston. As collector, he was boss of the customshouse. My mother took his twin daughters (my nieces) and me, then a small boy, to visit him once at his office. In those days the customshouse tower, at 450 feet, was by far the tallest structure in Boston, and its most familiar landmark. Following our greetings and inspection of his office, Wilfred announced he would escort us to the top of the tower, an invitation mother respectfully declined—no 450-foot tower for her! Upon arrival at the observation deck I found the parapet too high for me to see over, so Wilfred grabbed me and set me on the railing, the better to enjoy the magnificent view. It was wonderful. We could see almost all the way back to Cape Ann.

Upon returning to Mother waiting in the office, the girls gleefully described our experience, including my perch on the railing. Momentarily speechless, she exploded, "WHAT?" (The "what" expressed with crescendo.) "You mean to tell me you sat that child on the railing up there?" she shrieked. "How could you do a fool trick like that?" Then, feeling weak, she collapsed into a chair. Ever afterward she would blanch and exclaim all over again each time she recalled the incident. Poor Wilfred never lived it down. I didn't mind it a bit.

I must admit my camp experience was not all bad, for I did make some good friends, and I do remember a number of very pleasant times. As a matter of fact, I returned to the camp for one month in each of two succeeding summers. Anyway, the busses came the last week in August and carried us all back to civilization. Hallelujah !

In the course of a narrative such as this, I would be remiss if I failed to mention Sundays. They were special days. No work was ever done on Sunday in Father's shipyard, or for that matter in any Essex shipyard. After all, even if one didn't go to church, with a work week of six full days, Sunday needed to be a day of rest. Sunday, for me, was a day to get dressed up, to visit family and friends, to go for walks with Father, and to go to church. I don't think there was a Sunday when Father was physically able to stand on his feet that he didn't go to church, wherever he was. Moreover, he expected his wife and child to be with him as he sat in pew sixty-five of the Congregational Church. Before my time, my half-brothers and sisters had had their turn.

However, Father wasn't there merely for the sake of appearances; he was a believer and took the precepts of his faith very seriously. To him the Ten Commandments meant exactly what they said. I can remember when a skipper came to the house on a Sunday expecting to discuss a new vessel. He was met at the door and abruptly informed that, "I don't do business on Sunday!" Furthermore, I cannot recall that he ever used profanity. "Ginger" was his only expletive.

Father began each day, as I have said, by reading aloud from his Bible, and he was exceedingly generous in his contributions to his church. For many years he served on the governing parish committee. It is not known how many people in tough straits he helped out. I must say that my mother, in her own right, was equally strong in the faith, both my parents having been nurtured and steeped in the old traditions of Yankee Protestantism back to the time of our ancestors' arrival from England in the early 1600s.

On the subject of ancestors, half-brothers, half-sisters, and so on, my father's marriage to Mother, twenty-three years his junior, had created some curious family relationships. Of the eight children by his first wife, only five reached adulthood and, of these, a son, Arthur D. Story, Jr., died at the age of eighteen and a half years. One daughter died at five and a half, one at one and a half, and another son lived just over a year. So I had three half-sisters and a half-brother, all of whom were well old enough to be my parents. (Interestingly, two of my sisters had been schoolmates of my mother.) Their children thus became my nieces and nephews and, with only two exceptions, were older, some much older, than I was.

I cherish the memory of those walks I used to take with my father on Sunday afternoons. Here I was, a child, in warm rapport with a man quite old enough to be my great-grandfather. The fact of his parenthood notwithstanding, we enjoyed one another's company. I doubt that as a young father he had had such a relationship with his other sons; the years had mellowed him. In the warmer months we walked somewhere about the town nearly every Sunday. Nowadays, the places we walked so often are wholly grown up with trees and brush, but at that time our hills and surrounding areas were open pastureland populated by the cows of the thirty or more local farmers.

He had a particular aversion to tent caterpillars, and if it was spring and he spied a nest, he would stride over to it and thrust his hand into the fibrous squirming mass and strip it from the branch, wiping it off on the ground at his feet. I still cringe at the very thought of it. Another trick of his was to take my hand and steer me toward an enormous cowflap, only to hoist me over at the last moment.

The ancient stone powderhouse, erected by the Essex Light Infantry in 1812, was a favorite destination, as was the summit of Fifteen Tree Hill nearby. The name refers to the existence of three rows of five willow trees, all carefully spaced. From a distance, one saw three trees or five, depending on the point of observation. We liked to walk up the tracks of the Essex branch of the Boston & Maine Railroad where I would gingerly step across the bridge over the Essex falls below. I came to be familiar with many of the town's landmarks and to know who lived in most of the houses we passed. From my most tender years I have maintained a fascination with automobiles and trucks, and at a very early age could tell all the various makes. Father and I would often stand by the fence in the center of town to watch the cars go by, while I called out the names of each. We would frequently conclude our afternoon with the purchase of ice cream cones from Zillah Mess, and if my small legs were too tired to go further, he hoisted me to his shoulders and carried me home.

Speaking of the Essex branch of the railroad, it should be said that for over sixty years that branch was vital to the conduct of business in the Essex shipyards. Over it came millions of board feet of lumber and timber, to say nothing of all the freight for the rest of the town. Outbound, the trains took hundreds of thousands of tons of ice from our lake, plus shoes from the shoe factory and barreled clams. We had freight trains coming in two or three times a week and, until 1928, passenger trains four times a day. Much of our oak came from nearby New Hampshire and Maine, but really large and long pieces came from southern Ohio or the region of the Delaware Water Gap. Fir for spars and ceiling came from Oregon and Washington, while long leaf yellow (hard) pine came from the South. By and large it was only white pine, used for decking and joiner work, that was harvested locally. Some of the oak and fir was long enough to occupy the length of two flatcars, maybe fifty or sixty feet and sometimes more.

An ancillary business was that of the teamsters, whose job it was to move this stuff from the depot to the shipyards. They used heavy high-wheeled wagons drawn by oxen, and later horses, which they drove up alongside the freight cars and then rolled the stock from one to the other. They would come along the streets with the planks way out over the horses' heads in front and dragging on the ground in the back. It was no easy trick to come down the hill in the back of our yard and make a right-angle turn into the storage area. They would sometimes use a wooden billet stuck through the spokes of one wheel for a brake. Occasionally a load would get away from them, at which point the horses were on their own. Instinctively, they would make the turn at the bottom. The last man to do this, and whom I remember so well, was John Tebo. He had a voice like a fog horn; if he hollered in Essex Falls, you could almost hear him downtown. He was proud of his fine teams and handled them with consummate skill. For as long as lumber continued to arrive by rail, which was essentially as long as Father and Mr. James were in business, the teamsters brought it from the depot to the shipyards.

I have just referred to the use of native white pine, some of which was also delivered by horse and wagon. For example, the pine boards we used in the construction of forecastles came, in Father's day, from the Carleton Mill in the nearby town of Rowley. Until the late 1920s, Mr. Carleton sent his boards by wagon, a distance of some ten miles or so. The boards would be unloaded and stored in our barn at home on Winthop Street. It fascinated me to watch the driver as he backed his fine span of horses into the driveway to the barn. Now it's one thing to drive a pair of horses forward, but to back a team for any distance is something else again; also, the nuts that hold wagon wheels on are threaded to remain tight with the wheels turning forward, but sometimes, with the wheels turning backward, they will unscrew and come off. This is what they did sometimes backing into our long driveway—one more chore for the driver to contend with. Since the loads usually arrived shortly before noon, the driver would hang the feed-bags over the horses' heads and then eat his own lunch before unloading all those boards alone.

As a postscript to all this, I might add that the goings-on in and about the depot yard occupied considerable of my attention. It was fun to watch the trains, or to run about the platform of the station and the freight house, or clamber over the turntable or the snowplow that the railroad stored there. Many are the times I helped to turn the engine on that big iron turntable. Sometimes the engineer let me ride in the cab.

When I was a little older, sometimes Father would take me to Boston with him on his business errands. Inevitably these errands took us over to the Boston Fish Pier where several of his customers had their offices. This, I found, was an utterly fascinating place. Often the fishing vessels would be tied two and three deep around the pier, and many had names I remembered from the days I played on and about them in our yard in Essex. All about me was a hurly-burly of pushcarts, shouting men, boxes of fish, and those wonderful silent electric trucks scurrying about with loads of crushed ice. Before leaving the pier, Father would generally visit Uncle Jacob, his youngest brother, who was office manager for O'Hara Brothers, one of the larger wholesale firms, and for whom Father built a number of vessels. I was fond of Uncle Jacob, too, a very quiet, smiling type of man who liked to make me laugh. He would occasionally come to visit us at home and stay overnight. It always impressed me that he would never have a bag of any kind, but would come completely empty-handed. It was one of his sons who became the millionaire investment counselor.

Father liked to take boat trips, and inasmuch as Mother wanted no part of any boat trips, he realized, I guess, that in me he had a good excuse to take them. The first one we took was the voyage from Boston to Provincetown aboard the steamer *Dorothy Bradford*. I had never been on a steamer before and enjoyed the trip enormously. Father had built the steamer *Cape Cod*, which had immediately preceded the *Bradford* on this run and was in that service for many years.

Having tried the Provincetown trip, he decided we should take the Nantasket Steamboat Company run from Boston to Plymouth. It was a lovely summer day when we went, but the steamer was considerably smaller than the *Dorothy Bradford* had been and the seas were rather rough. I wasn't sick myself, but the sight of passengers throwing up over the rail was somewhat unnerving, and we both decided maybe it would be just as well to come home on the train.

The last of these trips was in September 1931, on the Eastern Steamship Line to New York. Along with me he took his grandson the aforementioned Don Goodhue. This, for me, was an exciting experience indeed, not only the overnight boat trip, but my first visit to New York. We had planned to stay a couple of days, but on the second day Father began to feel ill, and from similar past experiences decided he'd better head for home. So once again we returned to Boston on the train.

I don't remember how old I was, although it must have been after Camp Ossipee, but there came a time when I realized I needed a boat of my own, and so I began to make inquiring overtures to Father. I suppose that at length he got tired of hearing me and accordingly delegated Albay Muise to make something for me. What resulted was a ten-foot flat-bottomed skiff as elemental in its construction as could possibly be. When finished, it looked as though it was all bow, but never mind—it floated and it was mine. Naturally my mother was most apprehensive about all this, imagining, I guess, that I would fall out of it and drown in the first fifteen minutes I used it. However, I didn't fall out of it and drown, and in fact, I greatly enjoyed rowing about the river basin and nearby creeks at times of high tide. I used to keep it on the river bank behind the vessels where various of the gang discovered it was a handy thing to borrow if they wanted to go eeling.

This gentle world of mine came to an abrupt end at noon on Saturday, March 5, 1932, when Father died. I was with him when it happened, and a shock to my sensibilities it was. He had not been feeling well at the time he launched the *Carlo and Vince* on Tuesday, Feburary 23, and had driven down into the yard to watch—something he had never done before. He visited the yard only sporadically the rest of that week and by Saturday the twenty-seventh he took to his bed. Dr. Webster came and decided it was a recurrence of the heart trouble that had first occurred back in 1913 and which had been evident in a number of slight ill turns in the past two or three years. At the time, these were thought to be due to something he had eaten. In 1932 the awesome rituals that now attend a heart attack were unknown, and Father was told simply to stay in bed and the doctor would look in on him every day, administering the necessary medicine from his black bag.

As the week progressed, there were hushed conferences with Mother, and it was decided to summon my sister Margery Low from Hanover, New Hampshire, where her husband, Fletcher, was a professor of chemistry at Dartmouth. My other sisters were close by, as was my brother Jacob, who was running the yard in Father's absence. On Saturday morning Father signed a check for the payroll and received a visit from sparmaker Charlie Andrews, who wanted payment for a mast he had finished. Father asked me please to take my camera and photograph the launching of the dragger *Sebastiana C.* from the James yard just across the way from our own. I did attend the launching, but, for reasons now unclear, I did not take my camera. With pangs of guilt I reluctantly returned home, wondering as I went what I would tell him, for surely he would ask me if I had done it. I greeted Mother and sister Margery in the kitchen and with some trepidation climbed the stairs to his room. As I entered he was just slumping over—

his Bible, which he had been reading, falling from his grasp. With a shout I ran for the women. Dr. Ernest Steeves, the local man, was hastily summoned, but it was too late: Father was gone.

Harry and Luella Cleveland, our Essex undertakers, came and performed the embalming then and there. We closed the big roll-top desk and Father was laid out in the bay window of our front parlor. The outpouring of sympathy and condolences was overwhelming. A steady stream of townspeople, friends, family, and acquaintances came through our front door. Among the visitors were a large number of Gloucester skippers, several of whom were Portuguese and who brought their wives. In the time-honored custom of old-country wakes, they took up chairs and stayed—quite a while. Mother and sister Margery, Yankee Protestants to the core, were quite unprepared for this. With the coffin and floral tributes taking up a good share of the room, and these people sitting around, there was hardly room to stand in there. They finally had to wrestle up some refreshments. All of this with Mother in a dreadful state.

The funeral was held on Tuesday afternoon in the Congregational Church. It is quite a good-sized church, easily seating well over 400 in the second-floor sanctuary. The place was packed, with many standing. (Added to Mother's grief was her fear that the floor would collapse.) The Town of Essex added to this moving tribute when it voted, the previous evening, to adjourn the annual town meeting for one week out of respect for the memory of Arthur D. Story.

With Father's death, the management, and later the ownership of the yard, was taken over by my half-brother Jacob. Actually, Jake had been working in the yard since his discharge from the navy as a chief carpenter's mate following World War I. He had come along to where he was something of a lieutenant to Father. Not only was he competent as a ship carpenter, but he had good talent as a naval architect as well. At the time of Father's death there were three vessels in the yard—one a completed ninety-foot seiner, one a nearly complete seventy-five-foot schooner yacht, and the third merely a completed keel. The seiner, *St. Rita*, was launched March 12, the yacht *Jessie Goldthwait* on April 20. The keel became the dragger *Superior*, fully completed by Jake and launched on July 9, 1932. As it turned out, this was the last vessel to come out of our yard for two years. Coincidentally, the dragger *Sebastiana C.*, whose launching I had failed to photograph, was the last vessel to be built by Everett James. The Great Depression had come to Essex, and my world would change completely.

# 2

# School Days

With Father gone, my mother decided she no longer wanted to live in that big ark on Winthrop Street. It was an expensive place to maintain and especially hard to heat. The rooms downstairs were eleven-foot stud and upstairs they were ten. Closet space was terrible, and the kitchen and bathroom were primitive. From her mother she had inherited a nice moderate-sized old house on Spring Street, which she immediately set about remodeling and refurbishing. We moved in the first of September 1932. There was a shed and small barn attached to the house, and the whole was surrounded by a lovely field. Just across the street was another small field that went with the property. Altogether it was a splendid house and splendid place to live.

On September 7 I went upstairs in that schoolhouse on Winthrop Street to enter Essex High School. The total enrollment was eighty-nine, of whom twenty-eight were my freshman class. Having now become a teen-ager and one of the "upstairs kids," as we used to call them, I set about doing what teenagers did and being involved in the uncounted activities that seemed to embrace young people in our situation. For me, all thoughts of the shipyard and vessels just seemed to melt away—the more so since, for the first time in history, there was no activity in any Essex shipyard. Brother Jake had bought our yard from Father's estate, but he had nothing to build. The James yard, too, was empty and silent.

I must frankly admit that Mother and I were not forced to endure the hardships and privations imposed upon so many by the Great Depression. Though greatly diminished, Father's estate was still considerable by the standards of the day, and our existence was a comfortable one. Father had died intestate and, under the law, Mother inherited one-third of the estate, the remaining two-thirds being divided among the children. My share, then, was two-fifteenths.

The lawyer who handled the estate was Carleton Parsons of Gloucester, who was indeed a gentleman of the old school. A man of probity, he extended to us every courtesy and consideration at his command. He had no children of his own and went out of his way to be especially kind to me, often taking me to the movies at the Strand in Ipswich and bringing gifts on occasion. He decided that it would be a good thing for me to learn to play golf, so he bought me a fine set of clubs and arranged with the pro at our local golf course to give me some lessons. I felt sorry for that poor guy with me as a pupil. He did his best—first to teach me, and then to contain his temper. By mutual consent we decided to give it up—the lessons, I mean. I felt obligated to use the clubs and would attempt to play the course alone (nobody to observe). One day I fell in the water hole and that was the end of my golf.

I was not totally devoid of athletic inclination for I loved to go skating and swimming (thanks to Camp Ossipee) and to play tennis. Why, even back on Winthrop Street, I had joined innumerable scrub games of baseball. We sometimes played in a pasture with rocks or cowflaps for bases.

They even made me a member of the second team on the high school basketball squad. I played guard, and our coach, Joe Targonski, put me in often enough to keep up appearances, but the real reason I was there was because I had a car and a license to drive by then and would help transport the team. Somehow, as I think about it now, the idea of me on a basketball team is really comical. I'd go out there and wave my arms around trying to block a pass, but that's as far as it got. I didn't even know the damn rules. A treasured clipping from the Salem Evening News of the time has a group picture of our team with me in an EHS jersey. But wait, that's not all! On presentation day at graduation time I got an athletic "E," not for prowess on the field or court, but for being the manager of the baseball team. I was really proud of that E.

By and large my high school days were of small notice. I got reasonably good grades; I joined in all the activities—scholastic and social (especially the dances); I made good friends; I fell in love. What more can I say?

The educational facilities which that little school possessed were woefully inadequate. The available rooms were few and crowded; there were no laboratories worthy of the name, and there was no library or gymnasium. Baseball teams played on the town diamond behind the town hall, and the basketball teams used the auditorium in the town hall itself. The court was laid out crosswise to the hall and was about one-third the length of a regulation floor; the windows were covered with chickenwire. In spite all of this, we somehow managed to acquire a measure of learning and to have a pretty good time doing it.

As our four years of high school drew to a close, one event preoccupied us—the class trip to Washington, D.C. It was the quaint and ingenuous custom of many small towns in those days to send the senior class of the high school to Washington, believing, I guess, that it would prove to be a practical lesson in civics and that the young people should "go down and see where our laws are made." To pay for this trip the mothers of our class, by now numbering twenty-five, had banded together some three years earlier and proceeded to run a seemingly endless succession of suppers, cake sales, entertainments, dances, raffles, penny sales—you name it. They were eminently successful. My mother was president of the club.

We thought about it for weeks in advance. We all left for Boston the Friday afternoon before the April spring vacation. In Boston we boarded the steamer *Boston* of the old Eastern Steamship Lines. She left the wharf at 5:00 P.M. There must have been at least a half dozen other senior classes on board. Amid such joyful circumstances, the commingling of these happy groups was a sight to behold. Civics was not a matter of especial concern that night.

Upon arrival in New York we were taken on a tour of Radio

City, after which we crossed the Hudson River on a ferry to board a Baltimore & Ohio train for Washington. We stayed for four days visiting all the standard attractions including, of course, the galleries of the House and Senate, but, strangely, not the White House. Returning, we stopped off in Philadelphia to see Independence Hall. The steamer *New York* brought us back to Boston, arriving on Thursday morning. Needless to say, a good time was had by all, excepting perhaps our chaperones. What a pity it is no longer possible to travel between Boston (or Fall River) and New York by passenger steamer, that ultimate of civilized conveyances.

As the town clock in the tower overhead struck eight on the evening of Thursday, June 18, 1936, twenty-five members of the senior class of the Essex High School marched into the town hall to endure the graduation exercises and receive their diplomas from Paul M. Wyeth, chairman of the school board. We were the largest class ever to be graduated. As the town clock struck nine, we were on our way out. Sixty minutes and it was all over. Teacher Mary Durnion had planned it well. The time had come for us to take the first step into adulthood.

In my own case, the decision about what to do next had been made for me. From the time I was old enough to know what the place was, I had been told that I was going to M.I.T. My brother Jake had gone there (unsuccessfully) for a couple of years after enjoying himself at Dartmouth for a year, and Father determined that his last son would have another go at it and come out of there a naval architect. With his death, Mother had taken it upon herself to see that his wish was carried out. I don't recall that anybody had ever asked me whether or not I wanted to go there. As the child of straitlaced parents, I was brought up with the obligation to adhere to my parents' wishes instilled in my psyche. It is with considerable chagrin now that I look back and wonder why I didn't have spine enough to involve myself in the decision. Be that as it may, I accepted their decision for me to become a student at the Massachusetts Institute of Technology. It was, however, obvious to all, including me, that the preparation I got at Essex High School in the area of math and the sciences was utterly inadequate to deal with M.I.T. Therefore I spent a year in postgraduate study at the nearby Beverly High School, where I got some much-needed work in math and physics.

In those days, if a person received good grades in secondary school, he could be certified to enter many colleges, including M.I.T., without taking any examinations. The Principal of Essex High was pleased to sign my document of certification and I was in. I hasten to say that this method of entrance was one of the more unfortunate things to happen to me. Had I been required to take the old College Board exams, it would have been obvious that M.I.T. and I were not meant for one another. However, September 1937 found me in Cambridge among those august marble halls enrolled in Course XIII, Naval Architecture and Marine Engineering.

I should pause, perhaps, at this point and return for a bit to the shipyard in Essex where brother Jake, now the owner, manager, and master builder of the place, had at length succeeded in getting some vessels to build. As mentioned, there was no activity in 1933, but in 1934 he secured a contract to build a small fifty-foot tug, the *Joan Dunphy*, for a Boston dredging firm. Following her launching on August 7, the yard was again empty until early November of 1935 when construction was begun on a sixty-two-foot gillnetter for the Gloucester fisheries. Three months later a ninety-six-foot dragger was started, with yet another sixty-foot gillnetter begun shortly after that. As a result, three fair-sized vessels went down our ways in 1936 and, more importantly, a goodly number of the old gang were able to return to work.

Brother Jacob built a good boat. With his own ability to use tools, he knew how to direct his men and saw to it that the workmanship was good. He had been brought up in the yard, as I had been, and had had some valuable years of practical experience. During his time at M.I.T. he had acquired basic knowledge of the fundamentals of naval architecture. Combined with a good native talent in that direction, this gave him creditable skill as a naval designer. He had, in fact, designed thirteen vessels when working with Father and then designed several of the boats he built himself.

By talent, nature, and temperament, my brother was quite different from me. He was a very social creature, a hail fellow well met, and seemed to possess all the athletic ability I lacked. Dartmouth was the school he loved—a pity he couldn't have finished. In World War I he joined the navy and came out a chief carpenter's mate. He was later to become a bank director, a member of the town finance board, a member of the Republican town committee, a Rotarian, and an American Legionnaire. In marked contradistinction to me, he was an accomplished golfer who belonged to a couple of country clubs and was forever playing in tournaments.

He did, however, have a rather short fuse, illustrated, for example, by the night he was awakened to the squalling of a neighbor's cat beneath his bedroom window. He stood it as long as he could, whereupon he leaped from his bed, seized a brand new pair of golf shoes and heaved them out the window at the cat. At sunrise he went out to pick up his shoes; they were gone. He swore it was the Hood's milkman who took them. Another time he got into an altercation with a reporter of the *Gloucester Daily Times* who had had the temerity to print an uncomplimentary remark about him.

Preoccupied with my education and other things as I was, and since I was living in Cambridge much of the time, a great deal of what went on in Jake's yard escaped my notice. The evolution of my studies at school, however, rekindled my interest in the yard, and by 1938 I was paying more attention to it. On May 1 of that year, Jake launched a fine fisherman-type yacht, the *Skilligolee*, built for socialite Quincy Adams Shaw of Beverly Farms. She was about eighty-five feet on deck by 18 1/2 foot beam. Although she had more or less the shape of a Gloucesterman, she was to be rigged as a ketch. Mr. Shaw intended to use her as a swordfisherman, and so she had a tall foremast and a long pole boswprit with a pulpit on the end. Outfitted with tanbark sails and ready to go, she presented a fine appearance with good proportions and graceful lines, a credit to Jake, her designer. Jake had designed the hull; the interior layout and rigging were designed by Charles G. MacGregor of Boston.

The launching of this vessel was notable to me for a couple of reasons. Number one, it was the first time in Essex shipbuilding history, as far as anyone could remember, that a launching took place on Sunday. Number two, I suffered a most excruciating indignity: I was heaved out of the roped-off launching area by a state cop—for me something analogous to being heaved out of my living room. The cops were there to help the little Essex police force deal with the large crowd which had been rightly anticipated. Mr. Shaw had a slew of socialite friends and, what with the host of the curious who in later years thronged to see these shows, there was quite a gathering. I had invited some of my M.I.T. friends to come with me and see an Essex launching, but hadn't reckoned on a rope being strung to keep the crowd back. Accordingly, I did what came naturally and ducked under the rope to be down with the gang. After all, this was our yard! No sooner had I done so than a burly paw on my shoulder arrested my progress. Out! What a humiliation!

Alongside the *Skilligolee* another pretty little vessel was taking shape: a fifty-two-foot schooner yacht, the *Blackfish*, modeled after the traditional Gloucesterman and built for Mendum B. Littlefield of Mamaroneck, New York. She was one of architect Henry Scheel's early designs. She was lost some twenty-five years later when her iron keel dropped off while sailing in Long Island Sound. I kept close track of this project, following her progress as best I could from a distance, and then at closer range until her launching on August 1. I even helped to step the spars—done, by the way, in Essex.

Jake was to launch one more vessel, another sixty-foot gill-netter, on November 14. That winter he went to Florida. When he returned in the spring he wasn't feeling well. It developed that he had cancer and grew steadily worse. He died at his home on Maple Street on September 30, 1939. He was only forty-five, and though married twice had never had any children. Had he remained well and in the yard, he had promised to give me a summer job that year. I had been looking forward to it.

I knew it would happen. The surprising thing was that it

took three years. I went to the post office one fine day in June 1940 and drew out of our mailbox a communication from the registrar of M.I.T. In it he expressed the view that M.I.T. would have to get along without me. In plain English, I had flunked out. Thermodynamics, Advanced Applied Mechanics, and Economics II had joined forces to administer the coup de grace.

No matter how you cut it, this, for anybody, is a deeply humiliating and demeaning experience. No amount of rationalizing or "if onlys" can erase the fact. I can't say those three years were a total loss because they weren't. I did acquire a grounding in the basics of ship design; I did learn to be a ship's draftsman; I did become familiar with many of the elements of a number of sciences; I did encounter in one way or another some of the great scientific minds of the day. To me, it was a thrill to meet and exchange greetings with President Karl Taylor Compton as we passed in the corridor. Furthermore, I did have some memorable men for professors, men whom I greatly respected. I think of Evers Burtner and George Owen in Naval Architecture; Matthew Copithorne in English; Newell C. Page in Physics; and James Robertson Jack, the only full professor in the whole Institute with no degree.

An authority on the structure of steel ships, this dignified little Scotsman had risen through the ranks in the great shipyards along the River Clyde. All James Robertson Jack knew was, in a sense, self-taught. He was always impeccably dressed, wearing a wing collar and white goatee, and his obvious grasp of his subject, his gentle Scotch accent and manner of speech, along with a mischievous dry humor, assured that all seats were taken in his lectures.

Also on the plus side, I suppose, was the fact that I had done fairly well in my English and History courses, and the drafting. One does not, however, go to M.I.T. for its English and History courses. Perhaps most importantly, I made a number of lifetime friends. At any rate, with the receipt of the Registrar's letter on that June day, my period of incarceration was over and I was now on my own.

# 3

# Lyman James

In the same week that I received my letter from M.I.T. I got a job in Lyman James' shipyard, the only Essex yard in operation at that time. I was hired to be a sort of helper or general handyman, my pay to be forty cents per hour. The James yard and our own were the two yards to continue operations into the 1930s and beyond. It was situated midway along the causeway joining Essex and South Essex. The yard had been operated by members of the James family for well over one hundred years, most recently under the name "J.F. James & Son." Everett James, Lyman's brother, was the "Son" of J.F. James & Son and had been a shipbuilder of splendid reputation, as had the father, John Frank James. Everett's last vessel was the *Sebastiana C.*, launched the same day that A. D. Story died; Everett died in 1936. From 1932 until the fall of 1939 the yard had lain idle. At that time a growing demand in Gloucester for new fishing vessels was evident. Lyman emerged from a sort of semiretirement after receiving an order to build a ninety-foot dragger, thus reinstituting operations in the James yard. His first vessel, the *Governor Saltonstall*, was launched April 20, 1940. Work was immediately commenced on a second dragger, the *St. Anthony*.

It would be difficult to imagine an easier man to work for than Lyman James. Actually, he had been a grocer for much of his career—one of the two, in fact, who had regularly called at our home on Winthrop Street. He used to make the rounds in a 1915 Model T express truck. Coming along our street he would have as big a load of kids as of produce. He also

45

owned a group of boat storage sheds on the upper side of the bridge, and it was mostly to this enterprise that he had turned his attention when the grocery business petered out. In reactivating the shipyard he realized his own inadequacy as a shipbuilder and so engaged John Prince Story (no relation to me) to be his foreman. John had held the same job for many years with Lyman's brother Everett.

I remember Lyman as a slim, medium-sized man of rather angular features, with walrus moustache and steel-rimmed glasses. His usual garb was a dull-colored work shirt with a collar too large and always buttoned at the throat, an ancient vest of some sort, and a pair of baggy work pants supported by traditional countryman's gallusses. The whole was topped off by the ubiquitous cloth cap. His conveyance was a Model T sedan of somewhat later vintage than his truck had been. His face and expression reflected a benign and ingenuous gentleness of spirit. He was the kind of man nobody could get mad at. I was to discover later that some of his men often took shameful advantage of him. He was always a participant in town affairs and delighted to rise in town meetings where, brandishing the expense report of some town department, he would demand to know what the "miscellaneous" was for.

At the time I began work, the *St. Anthony* was framed and planked and the inside partly ceiled up. From being merely an observer of these procedures, I was now to be a participant. If memory serves me, foreman John Prince (he was never called by any other name) started me off driving long trunnels. "Trunnel" is a corruption of the word "treenail." For the uninitiated, trunnels are the wooden pins used to fasten a vessel's planks to the frames. A long trunnel is different from a regular trunnel in that it is driven all the way through plank, frame, and ceiling (the inside planking) instead of just plank and frame. In this case they were about fourteen inches long, not counting the head. It was my job first to bore the holes, then turn the trunnels on a lathe, drive them, and saw off the heads. Lastly, the outer end of each trunnel was split and wedged.

Traditionally, trunnels were made from locust. They came

to the yard as 1 1/4-inch boards, which were cut up to the appropriate length and sawn into square billets by the sawyer. The holes were bored with a heavy electric drill turning either a 1 1/8-inch or 1 1/4-inch trunnel augur. The lathes used for turning the trunnels were especially designed for the purpose. The one I used was reputed to have been the best any Essex yard ever had. That very lathe ultimately ended up in the Peabody Museum of Salem, Massachusetts, after being rescued from the Essex Dump. In turning trunnels the trick was to adjust the knife in the lathe to create a diameter that was just right—neither too tight nor too slack. If a trunnel was slack in its hole, it obviously would not hold properly; if too tight it broke in driving. One had to turn a diameter that would take eight to ten good blows with the beetle to drive. A beetle, by the way, was a large long-handled mallet. The heads of beetles were made from live oak or lignum vitae and were bound with steel rings.

I have attempted to estimate how many trunnels there are in the average ninety-foot vessel. If one assumes a two-foot frame spacing, which was standard, and nineteen streaks of plank, which was about average, that works out to 874 spots per side where planks contact frames. (I assumed forty-six frames.) If we now think of four trunnels per spot that comes to 3,496 for one side or 6,992 for both sides of the vessel. It's true that the half-girth of the vessel forward is much less than amidships, but the half-girth aft is much more, so it more or less averages out. Now it must be remembered that not all of the fastenings were trunnels. Galvanized ship spikes were used in working the planks onto the vessel, the number depending on the difficulty of application. From all of this it seems that an estimate of 6,000 trunnels for a ninety-foot vessel is not unreasonable. For larger or smaller vessels the number is obviously proportionally more or less.

Having driven a bunch of trunnels, it then became necessary to saw off the projecting square heads flush with the planks and then go into the vessel with an adze and trim off the ends that stuck through on the inside. Finally, with steel wedge and pin maul, the ends of the trunnels, both outside and in, were split and a small oaken wedge inserted and driven home. In all of this, the part that gave me the most trouble was hanging on to that little splitting wedge. If the maul didn't strike it fairly and squarely, away it would fly, and I would have to climb down from the stage and retrieve it. At length I got tired of this and finally tied a string to the damn thing, with the other end tied to a belt loop of my pants. It worked, but the gang got quite a kick out of it.

It was while working inside the vessel one day that I received a lesson in elemental physics regarding the transmission of forces. Ed Butler was on the starboard side aft driving through some long trunnels. As I stood idly watching the ends pop through their holes to the inside, I wondered what it would be like to put my finger on one as Ed hit it. I did. Wow! That hurt. He could just as well have hit my finger with the beetle itself.

That shipyard was no place for the overly fastidious. Drinking water was fetched in a bucket from a nearby well, and a long-handled tin dipper was used in common. When getting a drink it was usually necessary to brush aside a few wisps of chewing tobacco before dipping in. Considerable of the conversation and comment in the yard was of a scatological nature. I vividly remember working on the starboard side under the after quarter one afternoon when suddenly the back of my neck was being sprayed with water. Looking up, I saw Dennis Martin taking a leak off the top stage with me as the beneficiary.

The gang we had working on the *St. Anthony* numbered about fifteen to eighteen and was a motley crew. Many of those I remembered from Father's or the old James yard were either dead or had gone elsewhere to work. William A. Robinson, yachtsman and author, in collaboration with Howard I. Chapelle, had established a new yard in neighboring Ipswich for the building of historic replicas and had siphoned off a number of the better Essex ship carpenters. Others had gone to the boat shop in the Boston Navy Yard or the marine railways in Gloucester. Our gang was composed of remnants from both of the old Essex yards, including three or four good old-timers and a few promising younger men. The foreman and boss of this gang was the aforementioned John Prince Story—as I said, no relation to me.

How many people are there who live to be 101? And how many who live to be 101 years old do so without ever seeing a doctor? John Prince did! (He once needed a doctor to sew him up when he chopped off a finger, but that doesn't count— he wasn't sick.) When he took the job as foreman for Lyman James in the fall of 1939, he was eighty years old and had just become a widower. He was a peppery little man whose plodding gait belied an individual of extraordinary vitality, agility and endurance. A large and pompous fat man once looked at him and observed that he "could eat John right up." "If you did," snapped John, "you'd have more brains in your stomach than you've got in your head!" His mind was razor sharp and there was still a twinkle in his pale blue eyes for the ladies. Yes, and he never wore glasses. For their part, the ladies might have been somewhat put off by the seemingly toothless visage with tobacco juice running out the corners of his mouth, the ragged jumper, and the patched and baggy pants; but John Prince was not one to be bothered by trifles. He called a spade a spade, he had a caustic wit and some of his comments on the passing scene were at once acerbic and hilarious.

To all who knew him he was, and always had been, "John Prince." It must be remembered that for a great many years a large proportion of the town's population was named either Burnham, Story, or Andrews, in that order, and local custom and usage had adopted ways to distinguish among them. As we have seen, the most common among the many variations were the use of the first two names or the first name and middle initial. A native automatically knew last names from having grown up with it all.

The building of wooden ships had involved the whole of John Prince's life. His father, Joseph Story, was a prominent Essex shipbuilder, as was his Uncle Oliver, and I would assume that John had thus been introduced to the trade. A gifted man, he early acquired what appeared to be a total command of every facet of wooden ship construction. Although briefly in business for himself in the 1890s, he had mostly worked in a number of yards molding timbers, lining planks, serving as foreman, or more importantly, becoming general yard foreman in the James yard, as I have said, for Lyman's brother Everett. He had also served for a number of years as a town selectman.

To him I was "Daney," and before that summer was out he had involved Daney in many operations then under way on the *St. Anthony*.   I helped put in the rest of the ceiling, the shelf, and the deck beams, and then helped lay the deck. I became an expert at cleaning the chips, shavings, and trash from the bilge, remembering to holler, "Under below!" before heaving the stuff over the side. Our day began when the town clock struck seven.   Dinner time was from twelve to one, with most of the gang (including me) going home to eat. Coffee breaks were far in the future in those days. Afternoons were from one to four, and on Saturdays we worked only in the forenoon.  A number of the boys were what used to be called "fond of their tea," and would sometimes get pretty thirsty during the day. One of them would serve as the messenger and, when Lyman took off in his Model T on an errand somewhere, would "make a sneak" to the package store directly across the street, returning with a few pints of fifty-cent muscatel.  The storekeeper kept a running scorecard and was paid off on pay day.

When it was time to lay the deck, it became my task to "seam" the decking. I'll explain. Decking for the fishing vessels was traditionally native white pine.  It was sawn 3 inches by 5 inches and then dressed four sides to 2 3/4 by 4 3/4 inches. Before it can actually be laid, however, it has to have a caulking seam planed by hand from the top corners.  This seam is supposed to extend down only two-thirds of the thickness so that the decking, when laid, is tight at the bottom, but leaves a V-shaped seam for the cotton and oakum at the top. This is what I did hour after hour, day after day.  It's simple enough, to be sure, but it stimulates a certain amount of woolgathering as one does it, with the result that you suddenly discover you've seamed diagonally opposite corners of a piece instead of the two top ones.  It gets embarrassing when you have to stack aside four or five such pieces. To keep up with the deck laying, John finally assigned somebody to help me.

I was directed to go up and actually help lay the deck. This, I thought, was enjoyable. I learned to wedge the pieces of decking together and spike them off, after which I drove in the pine bungs (plugs) over the spike heads. There was a pitfall in this, too, as I discovered when I drove in a whole row of bungs one day, only to find there were no spikes under them. That's what it is to be a greenhorn. In the parlance of the old-time shipyard, a mistake of any kind, whether a simple one like this, or one of major proportions, was referred to as a "bull." A major bull might be one such as was made in the keel of the 610-gross-ton three-master, *Warwick*, building in Father's yard in 1891. The keel was laid and part of the frames erected when it was observed she was six feet too short. The keel had to come apart, and a new section was put in. The three midship frames were made just alike.

Years later, when I would talk to John Prince about the old days, he once said to me, "Ah, Daney, you know there never was a bull made so bad you couldn't get out of it somehow. There's been lots of 'em made, but you don't see any vessels left around here, do yuh? They're all gone!" A vessel in the James yard was once discovered to be five inches wider on the starboard side forward than on the port side. The skipper inquired of John how that could be.

"You see those cows in the pasture over there?" asked John.

"Yes."

"Well, about a week ago they got out one night and came over here and knocked out some of the forward shores on that side, and that's what made her spread!"

The *St. Anthony* had been set up in the berth near the street, and, whenever possible, I tried to be doing my work on the port side, the one next to the street. With luck I might catch sight of Margaret walking by. She, in turn, used to avail herself of any opportunity to walk over to South Essex, maybe to buy some clams, or get a pair of shoes fixed at Will Porter's cobbler shop (his name was Burnham). We had fallen in love. In August of 1939 her parents, Harold and Stella Bishop, had purchased the old Winthrop Low place on Western Avenue, and the family had moved here from Pawtuxet, Rhode Island. A few weeks later, while sitting in church one Sunday morning, I looked around to see this vision of loveliness sitting a few pews away. Happily, the following Sunday, there she was again, sitting with my friend Mary Barr, who lived across the street from this newly arrived family. I made certain to be there as we left the church, and friend Mary introduced us all around. In retrospect, I can say that with the exchange of a few pleasantries the denouement of emotional chemistry had taken place.

I went back to M.I.T. just about then, but found myself in Essex every weekend that fall. It turned out that Margaret, who had been an honors graduate of Brown University, had completed a year of graduate study at Columbia and was preparing to go back again to complete her master's thesis. She returned to New York in January, so the postal service was kept extra busy from then until June. She did contrive to come to Essex a few times in that period, which made it nice.

All of this may have been one of the reasons that thermodynamics and I were unable to hit it off. Coincidentally, Margaret seemed to notice that her interest in the thesis was flagging. When my notice of disaffiliation came from M.I.T., it took some doing on my part to summon the courage to tell her. She said it made no difference to her. Quite candidly, I had done my best to conceal the melancholy event, and my job at Lyman James's shipyard had provided a good cover. It turned out I was to get an even better one.

I seem to remember that I was wedging a few trunnels down under the port quarter one day in late August when John Prince looked me up to say there was a man up in the yard who wanted to speak to me. The man was John W. Hudson, chief naval architect of the Sun Shipbuilding and Dry Dock Company, of Chester, Pennsylvania, who was on a vacation trip through the Cape Ann area. In passing our little shipyard he had stopped in to have a look. He fell into conversation with John Prince, who remarked that there was "a young feller from Boston Tech" working there. "Let me talk to him," said Mr. Hudson.  The upshot was that he offered me a job in the hull drafting room of the big yard.  I took it.  I also popped the question and Margaret said, "Yes!"

# 4

# Chester to Ipswich

I left for Chester in the second week of September 1940. I was to report for work on Monday, the sixteenth, and wanted a day or two to reconnoiter the place and to find somewhere to live. My summer at home had proved on the whole to be a most pleasant one. The stigma of my scholastic failure gnawed at my consciousness, but Margaret's acceptance of me as I was did much to assuage the guilt. My mother would have forgiven me for anything, I guess, and was happy for me in my new circumstances, although I don't think A.D. would have been too pleased. In all honesty, I must admit that in my heart of hearts I was relieved not to be going back. However, my mother, by this time, was involved in a very serious problem of her own. A small lump about the size of a walnut shell had been excised from the calf of her leg back in the fall of 1934. It appeared to be benign and it was felt she would be OK. She was not OK, however, and within eighteen months it was back, bigger this time. Without attempting to give a medical history, suffice it to say that from then until March of 1940 she underwent thirteen surgical procedures for what, of course, proved to be cancer. The last one removed her right leg above the knee. Through all this, her fortitude and strength of character were nothing short of heroic. Never a word of complaint, denial, or self-pity did she utter, but with dogged determination began over and over to resume as normal a life as she could. She had entered the Salem hospital on the day of my junior prom at M.I.T. and wanted Margaret and me to stop by the hospital that night on our way so she could see how we looked. It was the next day that they amputated her leg, and she hadn't even told us! Here we were dancing the night away to the music of Glen Gray and the Casa Loma orchestra.

Being thus reduced to semi-invalidism, Mother was forced to seek a companion and housekeeper to come and live with her. The person she found turned out to be one of the most wonderful people I have ever known. In Ruthie Connor, Mother had the most ebullient and optimistic individual who could possibly be contained in one package. Moreover, she was an excellent cook and a good driver. She and Mother hit it off at once. If I were to leave, I at least knew that she was in the best of hands.

The Sun Shipbuilding and Dry Dock Company in Chester was an enormous place. Their specialty was tankers. At the time I arrived, there were eight shipways and a payroll of many thousands of men. I was assigned to the big hull drafting room on the third floor of the main building. There were about sixty-five of us in there. As many more were in the engineering section on the floor below. Our job was to produce all of the working drawings necessary for the construction of a 600-foot tanker. As I remember, the men with whom I was associated were almost without exception friendly and helpful to me. A number of them had begun their careers at shipyards in England, Scotland, Germany, Sweden, Holland, and Italy. It proved to be a great experience for me. For the first time in my life I had really left home.

At that time the region in and about Chester, along the banks of the Delaware River, was one vast aggregation of heavy industry. Besides Sun Ship there was the Baldwin Locomotive Works, General Electric, the Budd Company, Westinghouse, New York Shipbuilding Corporation, the Philadelphia Navy Yard, Scott Paper Company, Pusey and Jones Shipyard, and the vast oil refineries of South Chester and Marcus Hook.

To drive through these at night was suggestive of Dante's Inferno. Upon arrival I was fortunate, or so I thought, to find accommodation on the upper floor of a rooming house in downtown Chester. I looked over the room and it really seemed quite nice—clean and tidy with decent furniture. I had brought up my suitcases and shut the door when it happened—a slamming, banging, bone-jarring roar like to wake the dead. It was just a Pennsylvania Railroad freight train passing on a steel viaduct not fifty feet from my window. That viaduct carried the four-track main line between Philadelphia and Washington. I hadn't really noticed it before, but I certainly noticed it now. I bet there was a train across that thing every fifteen minutes. I was a railroad enthusiast then, and am one now, but this was too much. No wonder the room was so readily available. By a happy chance, a new-found office acquaintance told me of a vacancy in the boardinghouse where he lived, way up in the quiet area of Twenty-fourth Street.

By contrast, this was a considerable improvement. However, as time went by, it was obvious that Mrs. Glennie, our landlady, was not the kind of housekeeper I had been used to, and the cockroaches scurrying about my bedroom and the bathroom (the only one in a houseful of ten people) did little to enhance the picture. I had never seen cockroaches before. To make matters worse, Mrs. Glennie wasn't a good cook either; in fact, the food was awful. On Sundays we only had two meals, with dinner at 3 o'clock in the afternoon. A fellow roomer at Mrs. Glennie's was Gordon Carter, with whom I was to establish what turned into a long-time friendship. We both felt the same way about the place and decided we could do better elsewhere. Another office acquaintance suggested that we might like to have a look at a nice room in his mother's house. It was a nice room; it was a nice house, and Mrs. Grauel was a nice lady. We took it. I was to live there for the rest of my stay in Chester. Gordon, my roommate, was a junior engineer at the Scott Paper Company, the biggest manufacturer of toilet paper in the country. A University of Maine graduate, Gordon, a tall, handsome fellow, came from Bangor. It was mutually supportive for both of us to hail from New England. At least we sounded alike. We both took no end of ribbing about our accents. Natives would get us to say, "God'n Cahtuh went to Mistuh Hahdy's pahty in his cah" (translation: Gordon Carter went to Mr. Hardy's party in his car).

I alluded earlier to the cordial attitude of the men in the office, but one man in particular stands out in my memory. He was Andy MacLachlan, a wiry little bald-headed Scotsman, with the friendliest grin I ever saw. He was one of the first to greet me when I arrived, and he went out of his way to extend friendship and kindness to me for as long as I worked there. He introduced me around and was a big help in getting me established. In the office he often seemed to be everywhere at once. His specialty was designing and drawing up rigging, but I sometimes wondered how he ever got anything done, he spent so much time visiting all over the place. He had come to America from the region of the Clyde in 1902. After working in a number of American yards, he had entered Sun Ship in 1916. Early on he invited me to come home to supper with him. Here I met the genial "Mrs. Mac," the only woman I ever knew with orange hair. I really don't think Mrs. Mac ever saw a great deal of Andy since his availability extended in many directions, seven days a week. With wartime conditions in Europe, we were getting foreign ships in our drydocks and any time an English ship came in, Andy and others of the large British colony in Chester would see to it that the crews were entertained and supplied with cigarettes and other treats difficult for them to obtain.

From where I lived, in the 1500 block of Edgmont Avenue, it was an easy and pleasant walk to work. I had to cross the tracks of the Baltimore & Ohio, which frequently afforded an opportunity for trainwatching, but the last block or two before reaching the office was through an incredibly squalid neighborhood. Never before had I witnessed human beings living in such circumstances—an eyeopener, indeed. As a matter of fact, most of the city of Chester was a rather seamy place, with a government rife with corruption. Merely to live there was an opportunity to observe the seamier side of life at close range. There were four movie theaters, in each of which I spent considerable time. On Saturday afternoons you could go to one of them for a dime. Brownie's Sanitary Barber Shop would do a good job for thirty-five cents. Transportation into Philadelphia was quick and easy on the "Pennsy," or one could take an interurban car of the Philadelphia Street Railways, which ran down to Chester. Going by rail was usually easier than trying to drive in, for we did enjoy frequent visits to the big city as a welcome change of scene from the grayness of Chester.

Gordon and I had not roomed together for long when he received an opportunity for a good job with Eastman Kodak in Rochester, New York. I was sorry to see him leave, but by a stroke of incredibly good luck, another young engineer at Scott came to take his place. With Dave Gilmore I again established a friendship that has continued to the present. We had many good times travelling about that region of the country. I was certainly glad to have my 1940 Ford convertible, purchased the previous June. Throughout the fall and winter of 1940-41 I tried to get back to Essex as often as possible. My mother's condition seemed stable, but she was ever glad to see me. And, of course, Margaret was there. We decided to set a September date for our wedding.

I don't remember now how I came by it, but somehow I found myself in possession of an engraved invitation to join the launching party for one of our ships. I think it was on a Saturday in February, but anyway, at the appointed time, I showed up with all the high mucky-mucks, some of whom, I'm sure, wondered who in hell this guy was. We mounted the platform for the speeches and then cheered as the sponsor whacked her champagne over the bow. I thought it was great, though not much like an Essex launching. The next day I came down with the measles. Oh boy! I wondered how many of that crowd caught the measles from me.

In Pennsylvania at that time if you caught measles you were supposed to be quarantined, and a yellow sign was tacked on the house to that effect. My case turned out to be a light one, and in a few days my spots were gone. However, since my quarantine was supposed to last two weeks, I climbed into my Ford and headed for Essex, there to enjoy a quite unexpected vacation. I left poor Mrs. Grauel with that quarantine sign tacked on her house. For ten days I could enjoy Ruthie Connor's cooking and take occasion to call by and say "Hello" to

John Prince and some of the old gang at the shipyard. Margaret seemed not to worry about my measles.

At the office, I worked in a glassed-in section known as the Hull Technical Department. The guy at the board in front of me was a Dutchman named Bierstaeker. He had been raised and received his training in Rotterdam. The yarns he poured out to me about life on the Rotterdam waterfront would curl your hair. To the innocent country lad from Essex, these X-rated narratives were the more engrossing. It was his great misfortune to have his mother-in-law living with him, and his descriptions of their bouts of mutual animosity were appalling. One time he was gone for a few days. When he got back, he explained, "There, we planted the old bitch."

At the board ahead of Bierstaeker was an Italian, Tony Vettor, who became a good friend. He had come from Milan, as I remember, and had worked in the shipyards of Genoa. He was aristocratic in bearing and upbringing, and his clothes and appearance were always impeccable. I was telling him one day of the Italian families we had encountered in our business dealings in Gloucester and was shocked at his outburst of contempt for these *Sicilians*. In his view, anybody from the south of Italy was something less than human. My education was growing by leaps and bounds.

My drafting table was next to a window that looked out over a busy freight line of the Reading Railroad, and beyond to the city of Chester. I must say I did a lot of train watching, but as I looked out I also felt inwardly that a situation like this was not what I really wanted in life. Thoughts of Essex kept coming to mind: wondering what was going on in Lyman's yard, was John Prince still there, how far along was the vessel now under construction, etc. It was a sort of homesickness, I suppose, but also the feeling that it was wooden boats in my blood, not steel. I don't remember that there was at that point a consciousness of any desire to go into business for myself, but perhaps the seed of such a desire was there waiting to germinate.

When warm weather came that year, I got the urge to trade my 1940 Ford for something different. I was making good money, and had money anyway, so why not? With great pleasure I called around at the various dealers and at length selected a nice pearl-gray Plymouth convertible with a black canvas top, and skirts over the back wheels. I remember that on the night before I was to take delivery of my new car I stopped at the YMCA to have a little workout and a shower. The Y used to post mottos on the wall behind the desk, and, as I asked for my towel, I noticed the one they had just put up. It read, "He who buys what he does not need will soon need what he cannot buy." A twinge of guilt passed over me. The twinge soon dissipated, however, and the elation of my purchase put it out of mind. Little did I realize at the time how prophetic that would become.

By mid-July it was time to go house-hunting. I guess my lucky star must still have been there, for almost at once I located a splendid new four-room apartment created in a gracious old house on a quiet street in Media. The rent, as I remember, was $55 per month, quite a lot at that time, but I decided I'd better take it, for housing in the area was rapidly becoming scarce. Since I was now to begin paying rent on it I might as well live there, so I assembled some necessary furniture, said goodbye to Mrs. Grauel, and moved in.

The area now to be my home was as different from Chester and environs as night from day. Media, Swarthmore, the neighboring town, and other nearby communities bordered on Philadelphia's "Main Line" region, and were adjacent to some of the lushest and most lyrically beautiful countryside of any in the nation. Dave Gilmore and I had been exploring southeastern Pennsylvania for months—first in the Ford, then in the Plymouth—and were thoroughly enamored of it.

At the office, my immediate boss was a Mr. Roeski, the chief draftsman, who graciously granted me a three-week leave of absence to go home and get married. I left in mid-September, just a year from my arrival in Chester. For her part, Margaret and her family had been preparing for the wedding all summer.

Before a large crowd of family and friends, Margaret and I were married in that Congregational Church in Essex at 4 P.M.

on Saturday, September 20, 1941. I was twenty-two, she was twenty-four. Margaret was as cool as a cucumber, but I had never before been so nervous. My best man was Joe Quill, a staunch old friend from Beverly High days who had also gone on to M.I.T. The only difference was that Joe was an honors student who was to achieve great things in the General Electric Company. Anyway, he was there to give moral support, pass me the ring, and presumably to catch me if I collapsed. Our reception was held at Margaret's home and was a real nice affair. Unfortunately, the photographer Dad hired forgot part of his gear, so our only pictures were the snapshots taken by friends. These, however, did very well. Our honeymoon trip was through the mountains of New Hampshire and Vermont, to Montreal, and on to Quebec, returning through Maine.

Through all of this my mother put on a brave front and happily joined in all the festivities. She had made good progress learning to walk on her artificial leg, needing only a cane to get about. With Ruthie to encourage and help her, she looked wonderful in her new outfit. It was an emotional blow to her, however, to be losing me, essentially the only family she had.

On the first of October I carried my bride over the threshold at 5 East Fourth Street in Media. The next day I was back in the Sun drafting room for business as usual. Well, not quite as usual—after all, my circumstances were a little different now. Newlyweds, I suppose, live in a world all their own for the first few months, and so did we. Interestingly, we had two sets of newlywed friends from Essex stop by to see us on their own honeymoon trips, and my old roommate and now our good mutual friend, Dave Gilmore, dropped in often.

Pearl Harbor imposed immediate wartime conditions on our area. Security at the shipyard was doubled, and we went on overtime. Plans were made to increase the number of shipways and ship facilities. The Delaware River industrial complex was suddenly ringed with anti-aircraft and searchlight batteries. I signed up as an air-raid warden. We saved up enough gas coupons to get us home for Christmas. It appeared that my mother's health was beginning to deteriorate, and worse, we learned that Ruthie herself was planning to be married soon and would be leaving. This meant, of course, that Mother would have to find a replacement—not an easy task, for Ruthie's was a hard act to follow.

On Friday, February 13, 1942, Margaret's and my earthly careers very nearly came to an end. We were driving along the Baltimore Pike (U.S. Route 1) on this evening when suddenly there appeared a car coming towards us, weaving from side to side as it approached. We slowed almost to a stop and kept way over on our own side, but it zigged and then zagged right into us, demolishing the front of our splendid new Plymouth. The other car ended up on its roof in the gully beside the road.

It turned out that it was full of high school kids horsing around, with one of them leaning over and steering from the back seat. Miraculously, nobody was seriously hurt. Margaret and I were more shaken emotionally than physically. Insurance on the other car fixed ours up, but it was never the same. Moreover, it was only a few weeks later than a car running a red light smacked it again, right in the middle, with Margaret alone in it. Again she wasn't hurt, but I had to go to the police station and bail her out while the guy who did it just drove away. Such was the justice in Chester. This time, the accident bent the frame of our car, and we had to get another—a secondhand Dodge sedan this time.

As spring approached I began to grow tired of working in an office and considered making a change. My mother was beginning to weaken, and I thought perhaps I could get a job nearer to home. The Robinson Shipyard in Ipswich, Massachusetts (the town next to Essex), established in 1939, had grown and was now involved in building wooden ships for the navy. It seemed a likely possibility. Following up on a letter, I went to Ipswich in March for an interview with Mr. Robinson. He agreed to hire me beginning in mid-April. The yard was less than five miles from our home in Essex.

Mr. Robinson interviewed me in his personal office, a large room on the second floor of the erstwhile cottage that was used as the main office building of the company. My impression was that, in fact, this large room occupied all of the second floor. The layout put me in mind of a throne room. It was essentially vacant except for a dais in a bay window at one end, which contained his large desk. The bay window overlooked the yard. I seem to remember that a railing surrounded the dais in the front—an altar rail as it were. I would discover as time went on that this was wholly in keeping with the imperious figure he presumed to be.

That same lucky star was still there since, while I was home, I made arrangements to take the recently vacated apartment over what was formerly Grover Dodge's grocery store in Essex. It may have helped that Grover was a longtime family friend. In Essex, any dwelling unit less than a whole house was commonly referred to as a "tenement." I went back to Media to tell Margaret the news and mentioned that I had hired Grover's tenement as a place to live. Her face dropped a mile. "You mean we're going to leave this lovely place and live in a *tenement*?" I had to explain that the "tenement" was in reality a splendid eight-room apartment on two floors, with a pleasant outlook all around, situated right in the center of town. All this for $50 a month. I don't think she wholly believed me until she had at last seen it for herself.

I was glad to be home again, and I was pleased at the prospect of a reassociation with wooden boats. As matters turned out, the interval at Sun Ship was something of a bridging experience between two segments of a wooden shipbuilding career. I did a lot of "growing up" in that time. The drafting room experience would stand me in good stead when I arrived at Robinson's, and the associations with the many people I encountered were most informative and enlightening. I might say that it was just the sort of experience I needed right then. If nothing else, it told me I wanted no part of steel ships. I hadn't realized how deep my Essex roots went. It was an important period for other reasons, too. After all, it included our marriage and the establishment of our home.

I began at W. A. Robinson, Inc., the latter part of April. Perhaps we'd gotten our signals crossed, because they started me in the steel shop. I decided I didn't really mind too much since the experience would be good for me. The boats then under construction were minesweepers and diving tenders, and considerable steel work was involved. I would be doing layout work. As a matter of fact, the experience nearly cost me my life. I was coming through the open back door of the shop one day when a long narrow piece of heavy plate standing on end by the doorway was jostled in some way so that it started to tip over edgewise. I didn't see it coming and down it slammed, just like a guillotine. It missed me but took out the seat of my pants. Shortly after this episode I was transferred to the drafting room where I had expected to be, and where I remained for as long as I was at Robinson's.

Compared to Sun Ship, Robinson's wasn't even a drop in the bucket, but I liked being in the smaller place because my work in the drafting room involved me in nearly every phase of the operations. At the time of my arrival a program for the construction of twenty 110-foot wooden subchasers was just getting underway. A number of mine-sweepers had been completed and a 97-foot diving tender was on the ways. This was a wooden boat with steel framing. Anybody in the region with experience building wooden boats of any kind was almost guaranteed a job at Robinson's. As might be expected, there was a large Essex delegation, some of whom had been there since the yard's inception, and all of whom I knew. The yard was growing by leaps and bounds as more and more orders for navy small craft poured in.

Coming from a drafting room of nearly sixty men I found myself entering one with two—Geerd Hendel and myself. If I was to be paired off with one other man in a drafting room, fortune could not possibly have dealt more kindly with me. Raised in Hamburg, Geerd had been trained in the best engineering schools of Germany and was indeed a scholar, a gentleman, and an excellent naval architect. I was to profit greatly from working with Geerd. Major design work for the vessels we were building had been accomplished by the navy's Bureau of Ships, but frequently miscellaneous aspects of the design or layouts needed local amplification or clarification for the benefit of our own shops, and this was the sort of thing Geerd and I worked on. I was further delegated to operate the primitive ammonia blue-printing rig we used, trying my best to keep from being overcome by the fumes as I worked.

There were other "primitive" aspects to our setup as well. Almost without exception the buildings, hastily erected as they were, had a prefabricated steel structure covered with corrugated galvanized metal. They kept out the weather, but they sure didn't keep out the heat in summer, or keep it in in winter. On cold mornings, when Geerd and I would come into our drafting room, the temperature was in the high thirties. Imagine having to do your drafting with overcoat and gloves on! One morning our ink was frozen! In summer it was just the opposite. With everything wide open we could hardly breathe in there. The drafting room and mold loft shared the top floor of the main central structure of the yard. Below us were the stock rooms. Outside our windows on the water side were the four covered ways. All other ways, and there were a dozen or so, were in the open and all were occupied.

Presiding over the mold loft was an old Essex acquaintance, Marshall H. "Pete" Cogswell. Although born and raised on a farm, Pete had decided that cows weren't for him, and early left the farm to work in the James shipyard. He became an inboard joiner and a good one, too. Along the way he studied ship design and construction on his own. He remained in the James yard until it shut down in 1932 and then worked as a house carpenter, in the construction trade, or at one of the marine railways in Gloucester. In the late thirties he came to work for my brother Jake until his yard, too, shut down. At that point Robinson's yard presented a golden opportunity, and Pete went to work there, finding his way into the mold loft. By dint of a keen mind and great native ability, plus continuing private study, Pete became an expert loftsman, the importance of which to any yard cannot be overestimated. In those days before optical projection of patterns, and now computers, a mold or template of every piece had to be made. In other words, the whole boat and all its parts had to be delineated full size upon the loft floor. Pete did this very well.

I found Pete to be a remarkable man in many ways. In the

first place, his Yankee pedigree was absolutely gilt-edged. John Cogswell, the first of that name in our region, was a wealthy London merchant and manufacturer of woolen cloth who, armed with the grant of a large tract of land, arrived in what is now Essex in 1635. The Burnhams and Lows, from whom Pete was also descended, arrived at about the same time. With an agrarian upbringing extending back for generations, he was steeped in the lore of pastoral New England and Essex in particular. The melding of this with an astonishing spectrum of shipyard and other work experiences, gave rise to what seemed an inexhaustible supply of anecdotes and stories, many of which related to curious and humorous facets of Essex history, and which never failed to fascinate me. He was a good bass singer and a musician, too, and had played the B-flat bass horn in a number of bands. As a matter of fact, a splendid brass band was organized from among Robinson's employees a few months after I arrived, and Pete became an enthusiastic member. They rehearsed in the mold loft, which sort of distracted me from my work in the drafting room, but which I enjoyed nevertheless.

When the volume of construction in the yard grew until he could no longer handle the lofting alone, Pete was given helpers who seemed to come and go with frequency. Several could hardly be called balls of fire. One, however, was a notable exception. Most of us at some time in our lives are privileged to meet and know individuals of rare personality, character and talent. In Bill Robertson, Pete (and I) encountered such a person. A chief mate in the merchant marine, Bill was enjoying a brief respite from his regular convoy runs to Murmansk. He wasn't with us very long, but seemingly at once he grasped and carried on the work in the loft as though he had been doing it all his life. Bill was an extraordinarily gifted painter and sculptor in wood. I shall always remember the portfolios of watercolors he brought in to the loft one day depicting life on convoy duty and in Murmansk. The previous winter his ship and the others had been frozen in, and all hands had to spend the winter there. The pictures were done to help pass the time. One in particular was most poignant; it depicted Russian police shooting peasants in the back as they crossed over the ice in an attempt to reach the ships. The vividness of that scene as Bill painted it haunts me to this day.

Following the death of his father in Scotland when Bill was only eight, the family emigrated to America. His stepfather had dealt harshly with him and at the age of seventeen he ran away, to ship out aboard a Danish tramp steamer. At that point he seemed to have fallen in love with the sea. He had even spent two years on Admiral Byrd's second Antarctic expedition. One Sunday he took Pete and me to see the little forty-foot fishing boat he was building in the old barn near the house in Ipswich were he and his wife, Kitty, lived (when he was home). Kitty, by the way, was boss of our stockroom for a period. Torn as he was by a desire to paint and his quest for adventure and love of the sea, he experienced increasing emotional conflict, which burdened him greatly. He would die an untimely death in 1968 at the age of fifty-seven. When Bill left our mold loft to return to the convoys, Pete and I realized what an extraordinary man had been with us.

As the summer of 1942 wore on, my mother's condition grew steadily worse. Margaret and I lived just up the street a bit from Mother's home, so we could easily drop in every day to see her. It became obvious that she couldn't live much longer. It's a terrible and heartrending thing to sit by someone's bedside as they cry out in pain and beg—nay, pray—to be allowed to die. Mrs. Low, the wonderfully kind and caring lady who had come to be with her, did all she possibly could to ease the situation, but Mother had reached a point where massive doses of opiates seemed to have little effect. At length she lapsed into a coma and died on August 22 at the age of sixty-five. Her house, and what had been my home for eight years, now belonged to Margaret and me; so in September we vacated "Grover's tenement" and came to Spring Street to live, I for the second time.

Along with the rest of the nation, Essex was caught up in the exigencies of war and the war effort. There were no defense plants of any kind in Essex, but we did have two shipyards again, each busy building fishing draggers for the Gloucester fleet. Lyman James's yard was going strong, and my old boss John Prince had gone back into business for himself in 1941 at the age of eighty-two. That fall (1942) I joined a company of the Massachusetts State Guard, recently organized in town. This was the organization created to take the place of the federalized National Guard. Presumably its duties were to perform those services for which the National Guard would ordinarily have been responsible. Pending call-up for regular service, a goodly number of men about my age or older joined up. Age limits were quite liberal—among us were several World War I veterans. Massachusetts then being a Republican state, the lieutenant appointed to command the outfit was the chairman of the Republican Town Committee. He had no discernible military experience. Fortunately, an old World War I sergeant was available to get the show on the road and help the lieutenant get squared away. The uniforms issued to us were left over from Roosevelt's CCC; where they got the double-barrelled shotguns is unclear. We would drill every Wednesday night with the dear old town hall as our armory. Occasionally we would be out on weekends for a variety of training missions. The membership proved to be fairly fluid because quite a number were leaving for the regular services. At least when they got there they would be well indoctrinated in close-order drill, for we did become proficient in that field of military endeavor. We had a couple of encampments accompanied by "field manoeuvres." The experiences may or may not have had some tactical value, but they sure were a lot of fun. Anyway, we certainly looked great in the Memorial Day parades. Democrat though I was, the lieutenant made me his top sergeant, the second in command.

It was with considerable dismay that I received the news from Geerd that he would soon be leaving us to return to his beloved Maine. He had grown increasingly restive with the way things were done at W. A. Robinson, Inc., and particularly with Robinson himself, whose modus operandi was often a source of wonderment to us all. At times Robinson could be really strange. From his arrival in this country, Geerd had lived and worked much of the time in the Wiscasset-Boothbay area, and had decided he wanted to go back there. Another source of annoyance to Geerd had been Amos Leavitt, Robinson's roving deputy, a sort of glorified errand boy and general factotum who seemed to be everywhere at once, but never where you could find him when you needed him. They used to say that if you really wanted to find Amos you should go down to the middle of the yard and just stand there; in five minutes or less Amos would go running by. Be that as it may, I was going to miss Geerd with his friendly grin, the omnipresent pipe, and his reminiscences of Maine and Hamburg, Germany. His leaving left me in sole possession of the drafting room for a while.

For my part, I had very few encounters with Robinson. He would occasionally come through my drafting room, and I sometimes would have an errand up in his office. Once or twice he took a phone call in my room, carrying on a conversation in French. (It must have been one of his old Tahiti connections.) What I do remember, and remember well, was the time he invited the whole yard and their families to a supper to be followed by a showing of the shipyard movie he had commissioned. Presumably it was to be a portrayal of all of us and what we were doing. It's not clear just what his motives were in making it. We all gathered in happy anticipation at a hall in Beverly, I think it was. When the time came to see the picture, it was announced that the movie really wasn't ready yet, and so there would be no showing. What a bust! Why he got us all up there to tell us that, nobody could figure out. The movie was ultimately finished and some forty years later a copy of it came into the possession of the Ipswich Historical Society, which invited the public to see it. It turned out to be a fanciful and romanticized yarn about the establishment of the Robinson yard, and how some old codgers, veterans of wooden shipbuilding, were induced to abandon their rocking chairs and come back to help save the world for democracy. For the few of us there who remembered and knew these guys, the whole thing was hilarious. There was, however, some dandy footage in it of wooden shipbuilding. Where? In Essex, mostly, and at Waddell's little yard in Rockport, Massachusetts.

There was little or nothing about the doings in the W. A. Robinson shipyard. One assumes that, for security reasons, such
scenes couldn't have been taken anyway. Much of the Essex
footage was taken after the war.

On July 21, 1943, I stepped into a tobacconist and purchased
a box of S.S. Pierce Overland cigars in celebration of the birth
of our first child, a son, Richard Winthrop Story. We named
him Richard, after one of my cousins. Winthrop was just a
name we both liked (of course, it was also the name of the
street I grew up on). Mother and child did well, thank you.

At the peak of its activity during the war years of 1943-44,
the Robinson yard carried on a remarkable diversity of work.
On the three shifts, there were, as I recall, about 600 people
employed. The original order for ten 110-foot subchasers was
followed by an order for ten more, plus an order for four enormously heavy 110-foot wooden tugs for use in navy yards,
and also some diving tenders. Somewhere in there, I seem to
remember, were some small wooden transports that were giv-
en away under the lend-lease programs. In the steel department we built a large number of 50-foot tank landing craft
(LCTs) and subcontracted the building of sections of the big
LCIs for a yard in Quincy. To make the LCTs we developed a
very efficient assembly-line operation. All of this had grown
from a tiny operation built to construct a replica of a little Baltimore clipper, a realization of the dreams of Robinson and
Howard Chapelle. One of my jobs was to draw up, and then
keep current, a map of the yard. I was forever having to
change it as more and more shops and facilities were added.
Except for size, of course, we ultimately had all the shops and
facilities that the biggest of yards had.

The working boss of all this was a man who, when he took
the job, was seventy-six years old. Edwin H. Oxner knew how
to build boats of all kinds, and he knew how to manage a shipyard. He may have been seventy-six years old by the calendar, but the vigor, energy, and skill he displayed in directing
the manifold activities of our yard had nothing to do with his
age. He had arrived at Robinson's in the first place as a resi-
dent naval inspector, one whose ability and competence were

soon obvious. When Al May, the general manager of the yard at the time, became fed up with Robinson's and quit, Robinson talked Ed Oxner into taking the responsibility

His credentials were impressive. Born and raised in Lunenburg, Nova Scotia, Ed had worked in the shipyards there until coming to the States in 1890 as a young man of twenty three. He first settled in East Boston, working in those yards until coming to Essex the next year to work in Father's yard, building the big three-masted centerboard schooner *Warwick*. In Essex he met and married a local girl—a Story, as a matter of fact, distantly related to me. They bought a house on Story Street and began their family there. He left Essex briefly to work for George Lawley & Son in South Boston, but returned in 1897 to work again for Father building the steamers *Lexington, Cape Cod,* and *O. E. Lewis.* It was apparent that he possessed considerable talent as a foreman and builder.

In 1901 Ed established his own shipyard in partnership with my uncle Lyndon Story in what had been the old Willard Burnham yard in South Essex. Over the next six years they built fifty-two vessels, fishermen and yachts. At one point they had eight schooners lined up in their yard. According to our records, theirs was the only yard ever to launch two vessels on the same day. Sadly, the business failed, and Ed went back to work as a foreman for George Lawley.

The failure itself had some aspects worthy of note. I remember as a child hearing it said in the family that "when they began the business Uncle Lyndon had the money and Mr. Oxner had the experience. When they finished, Mr. Oxner had the money and Uncle Lyndon had the experience!" The implication was, I guess, that somehow Ed had gulled Uncle Lyndon out of his capital investment or that he had profited unduly. In fairness to Ed Oxner, however, I have been told that the principal reason for the failure was the "borrowing" from the business by Uncle Lyndon of enough money to buy a second house.

The last vessel they built was a schooner named *Richard,* which was essentially ready to go at the time of the failure. The vessel sat there on the ways for nearly a year before being wholly completed and launched. The planks dried out and the seams opened to such an extent that the Essex Number 2 hand fire engine was brought over to pump water into her until the seams swelled sufficiently to allow her to be launched.

Ed returned to Lawley's, retiring in 1934 as general manager of one of the country's most prestigious yacht building yards. In "retirement" he bought and operated a small yacht yard in Marblehead where he was when the war came.

It was interesting that, in spite of being born a Nova Scotian, Ed really regarded himself as an Essex man. His associations with Father and Uncle Lyndon, and having a Story wife, gave us an instant rapport. At Robinson's he used my drafting room as his office, always taking pains to be there at noon. He, of course, knew Pete Cogswell, whom he always called "Coggie," and together they would sit there at lunch time and reminisce about the characters and times of old Essex. What a pair they made—I loved it. I'm not sure they realized to what extent I egged them on.

April 10, 1944 was my twenty-fifth birthday, and one of my presents was a greeting from the President of the United Stated to Dana Adams Story inviting me to report for my pre-induction physical examination at Gloucester two days hence at 6:30 A.M. The point of assembly for me and the others so invited was the Gloucester depot where a kindly group of concerned citizens cheered us onto the train with coffee and doughnuts. In Boston an army bus carried us over to the cavernous Army Base in South Boston where the festivities would take place on one of the upper floors. Any illusion of grandeur, pride, or dignity a man may have are quickly dispelled when he finds himself one of about 200 stark naked creatures being herded from cubicle to cubicle like so many sheep. In due course we were all prodded, poked, squeezed, "aaahed," listened to, and questioned, after which we were put back on the train for Gloucester and home, there to await the verdict. It wasn't long in coming. In my own case I viewed it with mixed emotions. I can't honestly say I was anxious to go to war, but it was a severe psychological blow to be told that my country didn't want me. I was a 4F, they said, psychoneurotic with a case of hypertension for good measure. That was hard to take. I felt that, in a sense, I had failed again. To be sure, I was still enrolled in the State Guard, but in reality there was now little more to it than playing soldier. With the invasion of Europe, the State Guard was disbanded, so that was the end of that. They gave us a ribbon. I felt I wanted to be a part of something that was making a worthwhile contribution to society so I joined the Essex Fire Department as a wartime replacement. I was pleased to discover that here was a place where I might do some good.

The approach of summer saw naval shipbuilding activity at W.A. Robinson, Inc. reach and pass its peak. As replacements for naval ships, the yard began taking contracts to build fishing draggers. The complete designs for these were supplied by outside naval architects. Moreover, they would be built by some of the best of the remaining Essex ship carpenters, who knew what they were doing when it came to fishing vessels. In short, I couldn't see much of a future for me in the place. I decided the time had come to hack it on my own.

In May I negotiated the purchase of my father's shipyard and at long last began formulating plans to go into business for myself. In preparation for this, and to gain more practical experience, I resigned my job at Robinson's and went back to Essex to work briefly as a ship carpenter for my old boss, John Prince Story.

Some comments and ruminations on this decision of mine, if I may: I think this decision came about in something of the same fashion as my "decision" to go to M.I.T. From the vantage point of all these years, I can't honestly say how or exactly when I made it. It seems almost as if it was always there; that somehow, at some time, I would operate the shipyard—that I was expected to. Expected by whom?—A.D. I suppose, even though he was long gone. Had he lived, brother Jacob would have been running the place, but he was gone now, too. If the yard was to continue in family operation, that left it up to me. So I did it.

It seems as I look back on it that the sequence of events in my life to date had somehow dropped into place in proper order, that circumstances had conspired to bring me to this point. Was I possessed these last two or three years of a burning desire to be a shipbuilder? No. Was I now looking forward to trying it? Yes. Quite candidly, I was ill-suited to do anything else. Boats were all I knew, and besides, I had also decided I didn't want to spend my life working for somebody else. In sum, what led me to decide to become a shipbuilder? A process of osmosis, I guess.

# 5

# John Prince and Others

From drawing up high-pressure air piping systems to cutting in fish-hold bunker plates is quite a transition. One of my first jobs with John Prince was to help install the heavy steel covers or plates in the deck over each pen in the fish hold through which the crushed ice was loaded. John Prince and his grandson Jonathan had launched a new dragger, *Holy Family*, on July 22, 1944, and when I arrived at the yard in late August they were finishing up a few remaining jobs on the vessel as she lay at her wharf in Gloucester. As I remember, three or four of us went to Gloucester every day until these jobs were done. We were glad to be in Gloucester because the weather was uncommonly hot and Gloucester was much cooler than Essex. After putting in the bunker plates, we put the protective oak sheathing over the pine deck and came back to the yard to work on the *Tina B.* and the *St. Peter II.*

John Prince had again received an opportunity to go into business for himself back in 1941 and had decided to try it albeit he was eighty-two at the time. To help out and also to be trained in the business, grandson Jonathan was taken in with him and together they built a big dragger, the *Theresa M. Boudreau* in that year. To do it, they hired our old family yard from my brother's widow, Maud Story. Evidently John and Maud didn't get on too well (not surprisingly) and at the completion of the *Boudreau*, with the prospect of more vessels, he moved across the creek to what had once been the Oliver Burnham yard. Here they set up an operation of their own, and before the end of all building in 1949, John Prince and Jon-

athan, and finally Jonathan alone, built thirteen more vessels.
So it was in this yard, just across a little creek and adjacent to
my own, that I went to work.

I say "my own" for indeed it now was exactly that. What had
been the family yard since 1813 was now mine. Were I to begin, I would be the fifth generation of us to be doing business
there. Although the real estate was mine, a friend and I were
thinking of operating the business together. Philip Thiel had
been a student at the prestigious Webb Institute of Naval Architecture in New York, and for a required summer job in
shipbuilding, was hired by the Robinson yard. He worked as a
shipfitter, carpenter, and draftsman. It was in this last capacity that he worked briefly with Geerd Hendel and me during
the summer of 1942. We became close friends. Upon his graduation from Webb in the spring of 1943 Phil went to work for
the Colley-Maier Company, a firm of naval architects in Boston. He had elected to live in Ipswich, a place to which he had
become greatly attached, so Margaret and I came to see a great
deal of him, and together we began to think of what we might
do.

In the previous chapter I said I "had negotiated the purchase
of my father's shipyard." In reality those negotiations proved
to be quite complex. To my surprise it developed that I had to
purchase four parcels of land from no less than six owners,
one of whom was "an insane person." I had always envisioned
Father's yard as a single entity and to find it thus divided was,
shall I say, interesting. To be sure, he had owned the major
part of the land, but he had acquired only four-fifths of that
from his father Job's estate, and the remaining one-fifth was
owned by my Aunt Julia. Right across the middle was a piece
neither he nor my brother Jacob had been allowed to buy. Fortunately for me, the three heirs of the estate that owned it were
now willing to unload, much to my relief. One of these was
the "insane person."

All of this reminded me of the time my brother Jake, who
had been renting the land, became embroiled in some heated
exchanges with a representative of this family. I assume it all
started off with another attempt on Jake's part to buy the land,

2. This lovely summertime scene depicts the shipyard in which I did much of my growing up. We see the launching from the A. D. Story shipyard of the dragger *Ruth Lucille*, July 20, 1929. The launching pictured here was a typical Essex side launching, with ways only under the starboard side. Beneath the keel are greased slabs. Also in the yard are the *Donald* (left), which will be launched on September 23, and the framed hull of the *Elvira Gaspar*, to be launched October 23. At the far left some men are working on a new keel, which will ultimately become the dragger *Gertrude M. Fauci* to be launched on November 30. In the empty space between the *Donald* and the *Fauci*, a fifth vessel—the dragger *Babe Sears*—will be built and launched by December 18.

Over the trees at the left, is the steeple of the Universalist Church; at right is the Congregational Church. Obviously it's high tide as it had to be to launch all Essex vessels. Our average tidal differential was approximately 9 feet, ranging from 7.3 feet to as high as 12. The *Ruth Lucille* was about 98 feet long by 21.6 feet wide, and 93 gross tons. Although she was a fully powered diesel dragger, she retained the traditional schooner configuration and rig even to a little stub bowsprit. The masts, however, were short spars used only to accommodate the drag gear and to carry a small riding sail. By this date a pilothouse was routinely built over a fishing vessel's wheel. Transitional schooner-draggers like this were common through the 1920s. *(Photo by Edwin James Story.)*

3. This "Victorian pile" at 20 Winthrop Street was my boyhood home. It was built in the 1870s. Downstairs the rooms were eleven foot stud; upstairs they were ten. In a cold winter, it took sixteen tons of coal to heat the place, and in a high wind it trembled. For all its large interior volume, the closet space was terrible and there was no attic. Outside, as you can see, was an astonishing array of gewgaws and thingamajigs. In the backyard stood the splendid carriage barn of a similar architecture, which was a magnificent place for kids to play. The flagpole on the front lawn was made and erected by Charles Hanson Andrews.

The house next door (*right*) was the home of my uncle Lyndon Story. It was one of a number of splendid houses in town built by Ed Perkins. (*Photo by author.*)

4. My parents: Ruby A. and Arthur D. Story standing by the piazza steps of our home at 20 Winthrop Street. It's a Sunday in early spring of 1931. The boards they're standing on are there because of the mud. Mother, who has on one of her best dresses, was probably getting the Sunday dinner when I asked them to come out, and has forgotten to remove her smock. One can be sure that Father's suit was made by Uncle Lyndon, a merchant tailor.

Here's a pair of Yankees if you ever saw one. Both claimed *Mayflower* antecedents, and the first Story arrived from Norwich, England, in what is now Essex in 1637. We Storys have been breeding in this same spot for ten generations. *(Photo by author.)*

5. Here is most of A. D. Story's "gang" in the early 1920s. Twenty-six men are pictured; possibly a half-dozen others were not there to be photographed. I can count at least eight who are of Nova Scotian French-Canadian origin; two are Essex Burnhams and one is a Perkins. Probably only two of these men ever so much as attended a high school. In spite of this, they could turn out the average fishing vessel in about three months. The posts behind them are staging poles, which surrounded each berth (spot) in which the vessels were built. In the background is a vessel just receiving her bulwarks and trunk cabin aft. She'll be ready to launch in about three weeks. (Photo by Edwin James Story.)

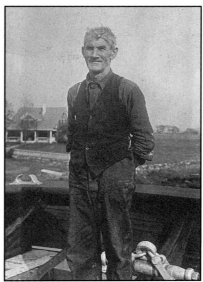

6. My father, Arthur D. Story. I took this portrait of him in the summer of 1931 when he was 76 and I was 12. Here he is with the "Roman nose" and the necktie tucked into his shirt. He always wore a necktie. He's sitting on the well curbing behind our house on Winthrop Street. As far as we know, he built more vessels than any other individual builder (or firm) in Essex shipbuilding history. *(Photo by author.)*

7. Jack Doyle, M.F.—Master of Forecastles. Few Essex shipyard men ever worked any harder than Jack Doyle did. In my recollections of our yard, he alone was responsible for building the forecastles of the fishermen, and could build one in an incredibly short time. He also had a prodigious capacity for chewing tobacco. His other shipyard responsibility was the launching of the vessels, a task he shared with another Irishman, John Murphy.

In this photo, Jack is standing at the stern of the yacht *Faith*, built for Mr. Weldon Shaw of Chicago and launched November 3, 1926. You can tell it's not a fisherman by the bright finish showing inside the transom behind him and also by those exposed knees. The device behind his left leg is a heavy spring-loaded sheet horse, which absorbed the shock of the main boom swinging about. These were also used by the fishermen. We sometimes referred to these as "snubbers."

8. I seriously wonder whether anyone in town didn't know Sammy Gray. A boisterous, jovial, ebullient soul, he was the sort of man to whom children and animals were naturally attracted, although he never married and had children of his own. After working for several years in the local line factory, which made steam-tarred cotton trawl lines used by the fishermen, he came to work in the shipyard where he handled the horse dragging the timbers around and also painted and puttied. Nobody could beat Sammy troweling putty into a seam. He was the only man who could get along with the sawyer, Liboire D'Entremont, and as a babysitter he got along fine with me. In the last years of his life he became a sawyer in the Lyman James shipyard, in which capacity he was serving at the time of this picture. (*Photo by John Clayton.*)

9. For more than eight long years the *Adams* sat beside Main Street in the center of Essex, her long pole bowsprit sticking right out over the street. Begun in September 1920, she was there until launching day, April 13, 1929. She became a frequent subject of newspaper feature writers as well as a popular tourist attraction. She even harbored a swarm of bees.

She proved to be the last three-masted wooden coasting schooner launched in this country. As Essex vessels went, she was fairly big, with an overall length of about 165 feet and a beam of 31 feet. She measured out to be 370 gross tons. Father started her on speculation in the short boom immediately after World War I. Finding himself stuck with her, he let her sit; nobody seemed to want three-masted schooners any more. After his other three-master, the *Lincoln*, was rammed in 1928, he finished up the *Adams* and sent her to sea. What appears to be grating in the bulwarks is the large freeing port just forward of the raised deck aft. The photo was taken in the winter of 1923. The ice shows it was a tough winter. *(Photo by Edwin James Story.)*

10. Edwin James Story. "Uncle Eddie" to me, he was "Eddie James" to most. I would say he was my favorite uncle. In the shipyard he molded timber, but his heart was really in his music. An accomplished musician, he played oboe, clarinet, and English horn. His second love was photography. The town is indebted to him for most of its early photographic record. He tried to photograph every Essex launching and would be seen lugging his five-by-seven wooden view camera and tripod all over town. For vehicles he used bicycles and an Indian motorcycle from which he once took a spill that nearly killed him. *(Photo by Edwin James Story.)*

11. Sparmaker Charles Hanson Andrews, known to all as Charlie Hanson. He made wooden derricks and flagpoles as well as the spars for the vessels. He used to say that to be a sparmaker, one needed a "round eye." He had a splendid tenor voice, and for a number of years was my Sunday school teacher. He was possessed of a virtually inexhaustible fund of stories related to his sparmaking career. His father had been a sparmaker before him.

12. My half-brother Jacob Story is molding a piece of timber, probably a keel piece for the yacht *Skilligolee* built for Quincy Adams Shaw of Beverly Farms, Massachusetts. Jake not only built the vessel, he designed her as well, along with fifteen others he built in his own or Father's yard. His untimely death at the age of forty-five cut short what might well have been a promising career in wooden shipbuilding. He stepped into the role of shipbuilder quite easily and naturally after Father's death and did a fine job managing our yard. He was also a good man with the tools; yes, and with golf clubs, too. *(Photo by John Clayton.)*

13. Lyman James was my first shipyard employer. A gentle and kindhearted man, he seemed hardly the type to run a shipyard. He had, in fact, been a grocer in earlier years. He was the last of the James men to operate their famous yard. His sister, Mattie James Head, and her husband, Fred, actually conducted the business to its final conclusion as a shipyard.

In this picture he's standing at the edge of Main Street beside the ways prior to the launching of the dragger *Ronald and Mary Jane*, christened, believe it or not, by Al Jolson. The date is September 4, 1941. The cloth cap and gallusses were part of his uniform. *(Photo by John Clayton.)*

14. This is Ed (Edwin) Perkins, working on the trunk cabin of the dragger *Theresa M. Boudreau* in John Prince Story's yard in the fall of 1941. Ed's workmanship was the standard by which other workmanship was judged. The smoothing plane and fore plane on the trunk top, and the short jointer in his hands, he would have made himself.

Ed was not always patient with the way old John did things, and no doubt was distressed at the quality of the pine John had given him to work with (look at those knots). We say "old John," but at the time of the photograph Ed was, himself, eighty years old and John, eighty-two. *(Photo by John Clayton.)*

15. In this day and age, one seldom, if ever, encounters a character like John Prince Story—"John Prince." I worked for him on two occasions. A master shipbuilder, he died at the age of 101. His whole working life was involved with building wooden ships. He was a master in the truest sense of the word. He did not neglect the obligations of his citizenship, however, and was involved in town politics for many years, serving several terms as selectman and (surprisingly) as superintendent of streets. Though seeming, perhaps, to be just an old "cranky Yankee," he had, nevertheless, a twinkle in his eye and a dry humor contained within.

This picture was made in October 1944 when John was eighty-five. He's standing in front of his shipyard tool shed and is wearing a Brown's Beach Jacket, the universal (in New England, at least) countryman's working jacket in those days. *(Photo by author.)*

16. Here stands a scholar. Lewis H. Story—"Lewie Newt"—never had more than an elementary education in the Essex public schools; nevertheless, he produced a total statistical record of Essex shipbuilding back to the beginning of government records in 1794, some 3,300 vessels. He spent much of his life at the task. He became a friend and advisor of Howard I. Chapelle and worked closely with him in his early work on Gloucester schooners.

Completely self-taught, he learned to design and loft boats and performed this work for John Prince Story. In this picture, ca. 1938, he stands by the door of his little shop, "Snug Harbor," in the backyard of his home. Here he exercised yet another of his talents, the carving of name boards and decorative scrollwork for the vessels. As might be imagined, he made beautiful half models in here as well. *(Photo by D. Foster Taylor.)*

17. What a pair! Tom Boutchie and John Prince often sat together in clement weather on the well worn front steps of the Essex post office. Along with acerbic comments on the passing scene, one of their favorite pastimes was the trading of insults. The picture clearly shows John's four-fingered left hand; a missing finger was the badge of a great many shipyard men. Note also that John wears a necktie. Those brooms behind the mailbox were part of the outdoor display of the general store, which occupied the other half of the post office building. *(Photo by author.)*

18. Walter Cox is putting the filler blocks in way of the foundation timber for the after gallows frame on the dragger *St. Peter II*, building in John Prince Story's shipyard in the winter of 1945. As a kid around my father's shipyard I was scared of him. Later on, in John Prince's yard, I worked with him; still later, he came to work for me. A bull of a man, he could turn his hand to any aspect of the shipwright's trade and do a creditable job. His greatest reputation was as the leading man of a planking crew, in which capacity it was common for him to put on two streaks a day on the average ninety footer. *(Photo by author.)*

19. Luther Towne Burnham didn't wear his political loyalty on his sleeve, he wore it on the front of his house. As election days neared, a variety of political slogans would appear where this one is hanging. To call him a Yankee conservative would be an understatement. On the Fourth of July, an American flag appeared that covered almost the whole front of the house. He had hoped to reach the age of ninety, as his father had done, but missed it by five months. *(Photo by author.)*

20. Father and son, Luther Edwin and Luther Towne Burnham "making in" the oakum under the turn of the bilge on what appears to be a fairly large vessel (judging by the width of the plank) in the James yard back in the 1920s. "Old Luther" holds and guides the horsing iron with its long handle while "Young Luther" swings the beetle. They're doing this to force the two or three threads of oakum well down in the seam. Before the day is done somebody will come along and put some good thick paint into the seams to cover and seal the oakum into place and also seal the wood prior to puttying the seam.

These men worked as a team from the time Young Luther began in September of 1912 until Old Luther retired in 1932 at the age of eighty-three. Old Luther, or Luther Edwin, as most people referred to him, was a caulker all his life, working on some 425 vessels in the course of his career. The grandfather was a caulker before them.

21. The author with most of his gang, photographed in February 1946. I'm seated at the right-hand end of the front row. There are twenty-seven of us here out of a total of about thirty-one or -two at the time. I count eleven old-time shipyard men in this group. Behind us is the mostly planked hull of the *Benjamin C.* She was planked with three-inch oak, trunnel fastened. The trained observer will note that we molded the bulwarks stanchions on the frames rather than put them in separately. I wouldn't do this were I to build a vessel again. They're too difficult to replace when put in this way. *(Photo by Norman Swett.)*

22. The author (*left*) with Jerry Hassett and Pete Cogswell standing in the shop door, May 1946. At our feet is a pile of navy surplus galvanized bolts. I am dressed like this because I have just returned from Rotary Club in Gloucester. I would later decide that Rotary Clubs were not my cup of tea.

Pete Cogswell was the first man to join our team. He came in July 1945 and helped to organize the yard. He proceeded at once to loft our first vessel, the *Benjamin C.*, in the ancient malt house in my father-in-law's backyard. Book-keeper Jerry Hassett was a man totally devoted to our cause. (*Photo by Norman Swett.*)

23. Bob D'Entremont at the band saw in John Prince's shipyard. He's sawing up what appears to be trunnel stock. The saw is a thirty-eight-inch tilting-table machine driven by a flat leather belt to an electric motor inside the building.

Bob's father, Liboire, had been a sawyer too, working in my father's yard. Few shipyard men ever worked any harder than he did. He sawed hundreds of thousands of board feet of timber and did it mostly alone. Bob was a hard worker, too, but booze was his undoing and he very nearly made it mine, too, when we launched the *St. Nicholas*. (*Photo by author.*)

24. This is how our yard looked in May 1946. From left to right are the frames of *Kingfisher*, the nearly ready *Famiglia II*, the framed hull of *Benjamin C.*, and the partly planked hull of the *St. Nicholas*. Above the scene is the steeple of the Congregational Church that appears in countless Essex shipyard photographs. Vessels had been built on this piece of ground back to the 1660s.

The picture shows our big wooden derrick pole, put up when we began. We would later have a steel one erected between the ways at the left. (*Photo by author.*)

25. The date is May 20, 1946 and foreman Albert Doucette and I stand by the stem of *St. Nicholas*. Next in line is the *Benjamin C., Famiglia II,* and the keel of the *Kingfisher.* Instead of the old shipyard horse to move things around, we used the Ford crane truck bought from the Robinson yard in Ipswich. It was the most useful piece of equipment we ever owned. (It's still in use forty-five years later.) The lumber lying on the ground is fir for ceiling, and the steel rods will be cut into drift bolts. Those three big cylindrical tanks *(center)* are compressed air tanks for starting the vessels' main engines. *(Photo by Norman Swett.)*

26. All that remains to do before the *Famiglia II* slides overboard is take down that ladder, smash the bottle, and saw off the way ends. The date is March 22, 1947.

One can see that putting a launching cradle under a vessel involves a tremendous amount of stock and a lot of labor. All of that stock must be fished out of the river and taken apart after the vessel goes. Of course it's even more work to put it all together in the first place. Expensive! A side launching could be carried off with less than half the effort, materials, and expense, and there would be little stock to be recovered from the water. We see here how the upper ends of the sliding ways are held by C-clamps and bolts. In the foreground is the big hawser that is attached to the drag. The name boards and stars up there were carved by "Lewie Newt." Before she ever put to sea, the name *Famiglia II* was changed to *Agatha and Patricia.*

The tide's in and the tug is waiting. All we need now is the sponsor. *(Photo by Bryant Burkhard.)*

27. This is an excellent illustration of how Art Gates began to get out a mast. He has taken a raw white pine stick from New Gloucester, Maine, and squared it up with his broadax, as we see. (The handle of the broadax has a slight off-set to the right.) Next he will hoist the stick up onto trestles and make it octagonal in section, still using his ax. Finally, with a drawknife and planes, he will make the stick. Bear in mind that in doing all this, he must maintain a proper taper.

Sam Parisi, the skipper of the *St. Nicholas*, stands in the background in this spring 1946 picture. Also in the background is the keel of the *Kingfisher* and our shop and mill housing the big band saw, the planer, and the trunnel machine. *(Photo by author.)*

28. The author stands in his shop door, May 1946. It wasn't my custom to wear a three-piece suit in the shipyard, but as I mention elsewhere I have just returned from Rotary Club in Gloucester. The box on the wall holds a fire extinguisher. The sign is self-explanatory. *(Photo by Norman Swett.)*

29. August 21, 1947. The author watches the *Mary and Josephine* take the plunge, and what a plunge! We see here the ground ways down which the vessel in its cradle has just slid; we see the severed upper ends of the sliding ways held by bolts and C-clamps; and we see the vessel taking a roll-down as it leaves the cradle. (It wasn't supposed to do this.) The crowd on the opposite shore was treated to quite a spectacle—more of a spectacle than I bargained for. Happily it all turned out OK. As a matter of fact, if we had given the vessel a real old-fashioned Essex side launching, it would have looked just like this.

Between the ways is the hawser attached to the drag. If things are figured out right, it will come taut before the vessel reaches the marsh island across the river. *(Photo by Norman Swett.)*

30. Along with George Story, our other caulker was Leonard Amero, shown here caulking around a stanchion on the *Felicia* in February 1948. Len, too, was a caulker of the highest reputation. An Essex old-timer, he started out as a young man working in Father's yard. When work was slack in Essex, Len would range as far south as Perth Amboy, New Jersey, picking up work wherever he could find it.

The picture gives a good look at a black mesquite caulking mallet. The head was bound with four steel rings, and each end carried a split designed to give the mallet a proper resilience. As the heads wore, the rings were driven back. From use in ship work, a mallet would end up caulking small boats. Note the typical caulker's wooden seat and tool box, an essential part of his gear. Note also the four-buckle "Arctics" that he wore to keep his feet warm and dry.

Nothing else in the world sounds like a caulking mallet striking a caulking iron. In Essex the sound carried over much of the town. *(Photo by author.)*

31. What we did looked like this when all was finished. Here's the *Felicia* built for Captain Sam Nicastro on an early trip in July 1948. She was our last vessel, the one that broke us; but she was a good vessel, nonetheless. She was designed by Pete Cogswell using the same model as *Mary and Josephine*. She was powered by a 400-horsepower Atlas Imperial diesel engine. She carried the schooner rig with riding sail preferred by the Italians. I was proud of her. In 1954 she was sold down east to Louisburg, Nova Scotia.

Oh, by the way, the *Felicia* was 105 feet long by 23.5 foot beam and measured 178 gross tons.

32. His name was John Doyle, but nobody ever called him John. He was "Skeet." I have no idea how he came by that name. Here he is using a portable jointer to bevel the edge of a plank. Such a bevel is planed onto the edges of all planks in order that they may lie fairly and smoothly against the adjacent ones and also to provide a proper caulking seam. In earlier days this was all done by hand using broadax and fore plane.

Back in Father's yard, Skeet and his partner Peter Hubbard (Skeet and Pete) were the outboard joiners who smoothed up the outsides of the hulls. There were no power tools to assist in those days, but a new vessel would have topsides, at least, as smooth as glass. *(Photo by author.)*

33. Here is Steve Price, one of our treasured old-timers. After a lifetime of shipyard experience he finished off his career working for me. He was in his eighties at the time. He was one of those who only needed to be told once what you wanted him to do. In the photo he's using his broadax to finish shaping one of the big timbers in the stern circle of the *Benjamin C.* in December 1945. From fedora to new clean overalls, his appearance was always neat as a pin.

Our big forty-inch tilting-arbor band saw shows in the mill door in the background. It was powered by a fifteen-horsepower motor. *(Photo by author.)*

34. The "granite-jawed countenance" of Charlie Conrad. Though not from a shipyard background, he proved to be one of our best men. A former dory fisherman, he knew what a hard day's work was like and expected to give anyone for whom he worked their full money's worth.

Here, at the age of eighty-four, he's digging a cesspool. The coming of Essex's public water supply, plus the introduction of modern well-drilling techniques, mostly rendered obsolete the digging and stoning up of dug wells. Yet, Charlie still did this type of work at an age when many men are in their graves. When I was a kid, he was always considered the strongest man in town. *(Photo by John Perkins.)*

35. I can say with assurance that George Story was one of the best and most skillful caulkers who ever worked in an Essex yard. As a young man, he started working for Father in 1922 on the racing schooner *Henry Ford*. Though among the best, and proud of his skill, George was not a prima donna. He would willingly and cheerfully perform any task requested of him and would do all he could to promote the interest of his employers, including me.

The two caulkers standing behind him are Len Amero and Frank Huntington. All three hold their precious black mesquite mallets. These, and all caulking tools in fact, were made by C. Drew & Co. in Kingston, Massachusetts. Mallets were also made of live oak, but most caulkers preferred black mesquite.

In this 1928 photograph, the author, age nine, is sitting on the staging behind the men. *(Photo by Edwin James Story.)*

36. This interesting view of Essex Center was made in mid-March of 1947, approximately two years before the end of all shipbuilding in Essex, and after nearly 300 years of an extraordinary industry here. At the left of the picture is the yard of John Prince Story and Jonathan Story showing the big dragger *Mother Ann* and the smaller dragger *St. Rosalie*. Across the middle is my own yard with *Salvatore and Grace, Mary and Josephine, Famiglia II,* and *Kingfisher.* Toward the upper right was the James yard, operated at this time by Fred Head and showing the little dragger *Bright Star.* The street that shows is Main Street leading to South Essex.

One can easily see the relationship of the yards and their ways to the tiny channel of the Essex River. It's about low tide here, but at high tide the river wasn't much wider. The length of the *Mother Ann* (115 feet) is not a great deal less than the width of the river. Through the years six different yards had occupied these sites. *(Photo by Norman Swett.)*

but in due course the talks became more and more acrimonious until the family put up a fence along both bounds, thus cutting the working yard in two. The lumber and timber storage was on one side of the barrier, and the building ways and shop on the other, with the result that for a time poor Jake had to carry all his stuff around through the center of town. You might say he bit off his nose to spite his face.

My sister-in-law's asking price for her part was a little high, I thought, and Phil and I concocted a scheme to see if we couldn't do better. We reasoned that the price to a stranger might be less, and inasmuch as she didn't know Phil, he dolled up real nice one day and with briefcase in hand went to her house to see what he could do. I watched from behind some bushes down the street to see if he got in. We both, now, thank our lucky stars that she wasn't home. If she had found out what was up—and no doubt she would have—we would have been sunk. What a dumb stunt!

The last piece I acquired was a small parcel up in the back corner, so to speak, which I was able to buy from an old lady, a member of the Choate family. This turned out to be an easy and pleasant transaction. Along with it came a small two-storey house in rather dilapidated condition, which we later tore down.

A parcel of land that Father and others had used down through the years was common or town land and lay between the private land and the street. In 1930 the Commonwealth of Massachusetts erected a memorial tablet there, which read:

Shipyard of 1668
In 1668, the town granted the adjacent acre of land "to the inhabitants of Ipswich for a yard to build vessels and to employ workmen for that end." The shipbuilding industry has continued uninterruptedly in Essex since that date.
Massachusetts Bay Colony
Tercentary Commission.

The "Ipswich" refers to the fact that for the first 185 years of
its existence, Essex was Chebacco Parish in the town of Ipswich. It was incorporated as the town of Essex in 1819. This
piece of land was roughly L-shaped and extended from the
street to the water's edge, where it extended northward along
the shore for something over 100 feet. Virtually all of our shipways were on, or crossed, this parcel. Since no other building
was then taking place, I acquired use of the land through a
lease from the town of Essex. The wording of the tablet indi-
cates that by 1668 there was enough shipbuilding going on to
warrant this action. Historians tell us that Essex shipbuilding
had its beginnings in the 1650s.

I hired a bulldozer in early July to come and clear the land.
In the nearly three years that the place lad lain idle a veritable
jungle of bushes and weeds had grown up. I cherish a photograph I have of Phil and me shaking hands amid the burdocks
by the old shop door. Bulldozers were not very common back
then, and it provided a wonderful opportunity for sidewalk
superintendents. I must say I got considerable satisfaction myself from seeing my land as it reemerged into view. A number
of interesting relics from years ago turned up. When Joe Vi-
tale and his dozer were finished, the place looked like a newly
harrowed garden waiting to be planted. It was my hope that
before long I might plant some vessels.

Although John Prince had Jonathan there, he remained very
much the boss of their yard. His ways were old-fashioned and
there were no frills to the operation. He was content to do
things the way they had been done for the last forty years. (I
was tempted to say 200 years.) As Jonathan waxed in knowledge and experience, he chafed under the old man's regime,
until at length the old man retired for the last time and Jonathan went on alone. That, however, didn't happen until after I
had left. Old John provided an absolute minimum of machinery and equipment to carry on the work. There was a band
saw, a surface planer, a small table saw, a trunnel machine, a
Skilsaw, and a steam box. There were a few electric drills,
some augurs, some screw clamps, and a bolt cutter. That was
it.

The gang was a diverse assortment, I must say. I can recollect the names of twenty-three men who worked there while I did, but various among them came and went so that at any time I don't think there were more than twelve to fifteen of us. Some were very young, some were very old, the rest in between. A few were really good men, veterans of the James and A.D. Story yards, and men who didn't want to work at Robinson's. Many were excellent workers, good mechanics, but had not had any great shipyard experience. In 1944 a little place like John Prince's would hire just about anybody who came along. Old John had two boats under way—all the yard had room for—and he needed hands to do the work. Parenthetically, the James yard was continuing to build, although Lyman had died that year. Management of the yard was carried on by his brother-in-law, Fred Head, a retired locomotive engineer on the Essex branch of the Boston & Maine Railroad. Their gang, too, was more or less of a pick-up affair.

Before long, John assigned me to work with Tom Boutchie finishing up the keel for a vessel ultimately to become St. Peter II, a 100-foot dragger. There can be a vast difference between an educated man and a wise man. A great many educated men don't really seem to know anything; a lot of very wise men have had very little education; some men are blessed with both education and wisdom. Tom Boutchie couldn't read or write, but he was one of the wisest men I ever encountered. Working with Tom became one of my life's more rewarding experiences. Here I was, at age twenty-five, paired off with a man of eighty-one, more than old enough to be my great-grandfather. Together we were working with Howard Woodbury who was in his middle seventies, and our boss was eighty-five.

I soon discovered that, though eighty-one, Tom could turn in as rugged a day's work as any man in the yard, perhaps more so. He had known hard work all his life, was used to it. Born in Nova Scotia in 1863, he began his career as a dory fisherman. In common with many Nova Scotia fisherman he "came over" to this country in the 1890s and settled with his family in Essex. He became a mason with our local contractor,

Frank Ellis Burnham, working as a plasterer and bricklayer for nearly forty years. He and Rose had twelve children. He told me there was a time when there were fifteen people at his dinner table. When work as a mason petered out, he went to work in the shipyard for his friend John Prince. Actually he had had shipyard experience before, working in Father's yard during the First World War. Tom exemplified the premise that a person of good native ability and a willingness to try could turn his hand to almost any task and do a good job. We saw this among others who worked in shipyards in Essex and Ipswich. Men who were really good carpenters (in Essex we called them "mechanics") could, without too much effort, become boat men. The same was true of other trades. Simon Doucette, who worked with us, had also been an expert mason, but he soon became a good ship carpenter.

Working with Tom was fun. He had a marvelous sense of humor, and his philosophical comments on the passing scene were priceless. He could match wit with John Prince any day, and usually did. He liked to tell me about his experiences working as a mason and how years ago he had repaired the chimney of my house. It was a good-sized chimney, and Tom had taken it down to the roof and put it all back up in one day. He was building a brick wall once and someone asked him if it was plumb. "Plumb?" says Tom, "it's more than plumb!" He did have a few aching joints, but he was sure the copper amulet he wore kept them from getting worse. He said to me once, "You know, Daney, they tell about the high cost of livin' that hurts folks, but it ain't the high cost of livin', it's the cost of high livin'!"

When our new keel was done and rolled over, Tom and I set about building the framing stage. This was to be the platform on which the frames for the new boat would be assembled, and it was built along the new keel. We spread out the cross members that went from cleats spiked onto the keel over to piles of blocking at the outer ends. With the cross members in place, we lugged over and placed all the planks to make the floor. It was a big platform; we worked all afternoon. When we had finished, Tom and I climbed up to survey it. "There,

Daney," he said, "I guess we can build a stage, me and you."
He gave a triumphant little jump and down went the whole
shebang. Tom and I rode down with it. We both had to
laugh. John Prince did not laugh. The next day we put it all
back up, more carefully this time, and we went on to begin the
framing of the vessel.

This, I found, was an interesting process. It involved the
laying out and assembling of the component parts of a frame
and then hoisting the frame into its proper place. Depending
on the size of the vessel, a frame is made up of two layers of
from four-inch to perhaps eight-inch timber. In our case, the
timbers were six inches. Thus, a completed frame was twelve
inches thick. The various parts are called futtocks, and each
has its own name. The futtocks are made to overlap one another for strength. There can be as many as sixteen pieces in a
single frame, all of which are fastened together with trunnels.

As we completed a frame, we would yell, "Frame up!" and
the rest of the gang would stop whatever they were doing and
come over to grab the thing and lift it bodily into its upright
position. Cleats and shores would be spiked on to hold it, and
we would proceed to do the next one. The stage that Tom and
I built was where all of this took place. One can see that as
more and more frames were stood up, we ran out of space, so
that we would have to take the stage apart and move it ahead.

The frames that we assembled on the framing stage were
known as "square frames"; that is, they were continuous members from side to side—a unit the width of the boat. It was the
custom to begin at the after end of the vessel and work forward. Since the shape of a vessel changes rapidly at bow and
stern, and because of the complexities of keel structure at the
ends, the frames in these areas were put up in halves, one on
each side. These halves were known as "cants," harking back
to the early days of wooden shipbuilding when they were
"canted" at varying angles to the keel. We assembled the cants
on a small platform on the ground at either bow or stern and
hoisted them into place using a gin pole and blocks and falls—
a laborious process, to say the least. The third member of our
framing gang, Howard Woodbury, was, as I said, in his mid-

seventies. While still a reasonably vigorous man, he was no match for Tom and complained a lot about the arthritis in his knees. He lived alone in Essex Falls and came to work every day in his old Chevy coupe. I did have to feel sorry for him when one day a kid who lived near the yard, and a real hellion he was, dumped some sugar in Howard's gas tank. It was a devil of a job for him to get it all cleaned out. He talked about it for the next two weeks.

I learned a lot that winter. At one time or another I participated in about every phase of the work except, of course, the joiner work and the caulking. Working all winter out-of-doors was an experience in itself for me; but it was only what Essex men had been doing for generations. My house was close by, a pleasant three-minute walk through the fields and over a stone wall. It was nice to be able to go home for dinner and have my little red-haired son come running to meet me. We had a number of northeast storms in the fall, which always seemed to coincide with a spring tide. This meant that Main Street over by the James shipyard would be under a foot and a half of water, and lumber that had been left too close to the river bank would go floating away.

When Tom, Howard, and I finished our framing, Old John put me into the vessel alongside to help with the ceiling. If I had thought framing was rather fun, I can say there was precious little fun to this. I had had a brief taste of ceiling when I worked for Lyman, but only at the end of the job and working with a large crew. Here I was to start from scratch and work all the way up. There were four of us to do it: Leander Doucette, Simon Doucette, "Snipe" Gosbee, and me. At least I would have three good men to work with. Leander was without doubt one of the best ship carpenters in the whole gang, a man of long experience.

Ceiling is the name applied to the inside planking of a vessel. (It has always seemed to me that it should be "sealing.") As it was in our case, fir was generally used for ceiling. Ours was two inches and three inches thick. Fir is by no means as heavy as oak, but it comes in long lengths—thirty feet or more. Every piece we used had to be carried on our shoulders up the brow to the top stage and passed through the frame timbers into the boat. It made one wonder if it wouldn't have been better to be born a jackass in the first place. We would pass in a number of pieces to provide a supply for a while, rather than come outside every time we needed a fresh one.

As might be imagined, we started at the bottom and worked up. In order to leave a proper space for ventilation, however, the ceiling does not go all the way to the keelson. Having established where the first streak would go, it then became largely a matter of "boarding her in" from there on. It is not necessary that ceiling be lined out as carefully and in the same way as the outside planking. It is there to give strength to the ship and to give a smooth surface to the inside of the hull. To allow for the changing shape and curvature of the hull, we would put in tapering pieces at bow and stern with every second or third streak. The ceiling planks were fastened in place with four-inch, five-inch, or six-inch galvanized ship spikes.

Now, all of this sounds fairly simple to tell about it, but when you come to do it, it's something else again. It means working up and down the inside curvature of the vessel with no place to stand except on the slanting frames; it's sort of like working inside a soup dish. Leander and Snipe took pride, it seemed, in trying to see how high up we could go before ultimately building a stage to work from. Also, to make matters worse, we couldn't use the ordinary heavy C-clamps to work the planks in because the boat was planked on the outside and so there was no place to hook one. The alternative was to use a specially devised clamp called a "ginney" (soft G). Many times they would pop out just as a heavy strain came on them and we would have to start all over. Also, fir tends to be rather brittle, and often, as we worked a plank into the curvature of the bow, perhaps, and had it fastened off, it would suddenly start to crack, and with a report like a rifle it would bust altogether. Once more we would have to take it down and start over. (Ceiling planks were seldom steamed to be more pliable.) What I have described was bad enough for two-inch planks but even worse for the three-inch ones. A cracking plank would never fail to elicit from Snipe his comment that "as long as she cracks she holds!"— a non sequitur at best.

Throughout the winter we worked a full six-day week. The weather was not too severe, but we did have a fair amount of snow, and the ice on the river reached a good foot or more in thickness. Shipyard men of Essex needed to work as many days as possible since, of necessity, a good deal of time was lost because of inclement weather. Two or three of the fellows, however, would get so dry by Saturday noon that they simply had to leave and go in search of something to slake their thirst. We had one, a French-Canadian named Alphonse LeBlanc, who disappeared one forenoon only to show up after dinner sound asleep out on the ice of the river. He used to assure us over and over that he was the best dubber (adze man) in the yard, even better than Leander (who really was the best). His parentage was most unusual, too: he claimed his "fadder" was a band saw (accent on the saw) and his "mudder" was a broad-axe (accent on the axe).

There was, of course, no such thing as a crane or a derrick in the yard. Whatever was moved we picked up bodily and carried. We firmly believed that Old John felt it was good for us to have to climb over piles of lumber and miscellaneous trash as we lugged. A bunch of us stood one day contemplating a heavy deck beam that, like all the rest, was to be carried up the brow of the staging to the topsides of the vessel. After watching us a moment he hollered, "Come on, boys, you fellers ain't gonna LOOK it up there!" One day the steel handle of the bolt cutter slipped out of its socket and conked Bill Stillman over the head. As he lay stunned upon the ground, John ambled over, looked at him, spat, and observed, "I guess he'll be all right. He ain't bleedin' any."

Speaking of bleeding grimly reminds me of a most unpleasant and regrettable incident that I experienced in John's yard. One of the gang was a little man named Joe Cooney, an untidy know-it-all type whose education, I guess, had not gone beyond elementary school. He had no particular skill and worked mostly painting and puttying and as a general handyman. He must have been about sixty. For whatever reasons, he took an especial dislike to me and enjoyed taunting me about not being in the service (he was not the first one to do that, by the way). I went into the little mill building one morning to turn some trunnels and Joe was in there standing in front of the lathe. He displayed a particular disinclination to move, and when I finally elbowed him out of the way, he grabbed a long trunnel and began to lay onto my head with it. In a semiconscious daze I remember looking at the patch of sunlight on the floor through the blood streaming down my face. They took me to get stitched up and Joe was banished from the yard.

Now that I both lived and worked in Essex, I was in a position to answer all the alarms of fire. Jonathan and one or two others in the our yard also were firemen, and when the siren on the Winthrop Street schoolhouse blew, we would all leap into Jonathan's car and be off. The first ones to arrive at the engine house got to drive the trucks, so we were anxious to get there quickly. Since the firehouse was only a short distance away, we would usually get at least one of the three trucks. Few things in this earthly realm can impart the feeling of omnipotence that driving a fire truck does. At least you don't know until you get there what sort of a mess you'll be in. Outdoor burning was not regulated back then, and when spring came and people began to burn their grass and brush, we were kept hopping. Not infrequently they would set their buildings afire. I also learned that hanging on the side or back of a fire truck in zero degree weather is no fun at all.

Back in chapter 1, I spoke of how, as a boy, I sat in the shop of Father's yard and watched Ed Perkins preparing the joiner work for the vessels. Here, maybe fifteen or more years later, the man doing the joiner work was Ed Perkins. They always used to say that Ed's work was the standard by which all other joiner work was judged. Now, at eighty-three years of age, that standard still obtained. Ed had always believed, and still did, that any job worth doing at all was worth doing well. Once a man assigned to work with him inquired how good a job he should do. "You do the very best you can," said Ed, "and when you get it done it won't be any better than it ought to be!" He also observed that, "When you hear a man say,

'There, that's good enough,' you can make up your mind it's a damn poor job."

Though, of course, it had at no time ever been formally stated, there was in fact a hierarchy among the men of a shipyard. At the top were the inboard joiners and maybe the men who could mold timber or line plank, ranging down to the ones who puttied and painted or the greenhorn helper at the bottom. An old-fashioned shipyard expression had it that "any damn fool can paint." Even among inboard joiners there was a distinction. First, was the man who built the main cabin trunk and after cabin; second was the man who built the forecastles.

Back in Father's yard of the 1920s and now in this one, the top man was Ed Perkins. He had learned his trade working with his father building cabins and forecastles, and had followed it all his life. They had their own shop in their back yard where they got out a lot of the joiner work using planes of all sorts they had made themselves. Ed could join two pieces of wood in an almost invisible joint. In slow times he would build houses, one of which was my Uncle Lyndon's. He made many items of beautiful furniture, including a grandfather's clock and another clock with wooden works. In my bedroom is a magnificent cedar chest made by Ed Perkins, an ever present reminder of the work he could do.

It seemed appropriate, somehow, that Ed and John Prince, these two contemporary old veterans of Essex shipyards, should be winding up their careers together. Each had an enormous respect for the other. One day years later, long after I had worked with them, I was visiting with Ed at his home in Essex Falls when he said he'd like to see John Prince again. I said I'd see what I could do and went to see John to ask if he would go. I told him I'd be glad to take him up there. "Oh, I suppose so," said John, "but I know what he wants. He wants to talk about old times. You know, Daney, you can't live in the past. You've got to look ahead!" Each of these men died in 1960; Ed at the age of 99 and John Prince at 101. Tom Boutchie died two years later at 99. His obituary listed as survivors nine children, nineteen grandchildren, thirty-three great-grandchildren, and four great-great-grand-children.

Of the fourteen vessels built by John and/or Jonathan, eleven of them, including the *St. Peter II* and *Tina B.* that I worked on, were designed by my distant cousin Lewis H. Story (also no relation to John Prince). Lewis's father was Newton Story, a half-brother to my grandfather Job; Lewis, therefore, was known to all as "Lewie Newt," or just "Lew." Design in our case meant "lines," and that's all. Lew developed the lines drawings based upon what the skippers said they wanted and what seemed to him to be good proportions. There was really no need of construction plans; John knew what the structure ought to be, and the skippers told him what they wanted for a layout and where they wanted bulkheads and hatches. What more was necessary except maybe a drawing of the main engine so that beds and shaft-log could be planned? Having developed the lines, Lew then performed all the lofting and made the molds. He did this in the upstairs chamber of Roy Burnham's barn, diagonally across the street from the yard. When the vessels were ready, it was Lew who carved in the name and port of hail on bow and stern, another skill in which he was remarkably proficient.

He was a middle-sized man, not too rugged, and of a quiet and rather shy demeanor. His pleasant face was characterized by his enormous bushy black eyebrows. Lew was yet another example of the self-taught man, the man of intelligence and dedication of purpose. He never so much as went to high school, but he attained such stature as an authority on the history of Essex ships and shipbuilding that no less a figure than Howard I. Chapelle came to rely heavily on his knowledge. They became close friends. He and Lew unearthed and redeveloped the lines and plans of scores of Essex vessels back over the years. Lew became obsessed with the idea of collecting as complete a record as was humanly possible of all the vessels that had been built in Essex. He literally devoted his lifetime to this task, picking out of government records the names and dimensions of nearly 3,300 Essex ships, going back to the beginnings of record-keeping in the 1790s. There were doubtless hundreds more in the years prior to this of which no record was kept. An old bachelor, Lew lived with his sister in the family home right on the town square. He had a little shop in the back, "Snug Harbor" he called it, where he made ship models—half models and full models. Using pieces of pine board, he carved and painted beautiful little bas-reliefs of Essex schooners plowing along under full sail. But it was the record-keeping that seemed to dominate his consciousness. Whenever I stopped over to see him, or even when I met him on the street, he would invariably talk about his vessel lists. Happily, they have been well preserved.

While it seemed appropriate, indeed, that we had five Storys working in a Story shipyard (I haven't mentioned Harry Story, distantly related to me but not John Prince), it was also appropriate that we would have at least one Burnham. He was our caulker, Luther Towne Burnham, scion of one of Essex's oldest and proudest families—also the most numerous. Born in 1891, he went to work as a caulker in September 1912 on the schooner *Yucatan* building in Leonard MacKenzie's yard in South Essex where his father, Luther Edwin Burnham, was then caulking. Father and son worked as an inseparable team until the last vessel was launched from Everett James's yard in 1932. At that point, and by then eighty-three years old, Luther Edwin retired. In his career the old man worked on 425 vessels, most all of them in Essex yards. He remarked that when he began, his pay was $1.20 per day.

"Young Luther," as everyone called him, carried on alone working in whatever Essex yard had vessels in progress. He had caulked for my brother Jacob, for Lyman James, and now for John Prince. Alone among caulkers, he would caulk decks working on his knees instead of sitting on the traditional sliding tool box. He was a loner in every other way, too, maintaining a lifestyle straight out of the nineteenth century. A little man—he couldn't have weighed over 125 pounds—he had never married and had always lived with his parents. I don't imagine he had ever entertained a heart interest, nor could he so much as drive an automobile. I got to know him very well in later years and visited him from time to time at his home.

To go into that house was itself an experience. I would guess it had never been swept or dusted since his father died in 1941 (his mother had died some years before), and all about were piles of old newspapers and magazines that he never threw out. There was literally no place to sit down except by pulling out one corner of the piano bench; the piano, of course, hadn't been touched by anyone in years. His bed was a dirty cot in the corner suitable, perhaps, for a hound dog. There was no telephone, radio, or TV, nor did the house have a bathroom. He used to say he couldn't have a bathroom because there was no way to install it over the kitchen. "You have to have a bathroom over the kitchen," he assured me. The place was heated by an old one-pipe hot air furnace in the cellar and by a magnificent cast iron range in the kitchen. Most of his fuel was scrap wood he picked from the town dump and brought home in a wheelbarrow. But he surely liked it hot in there; you stepped through the back door and it was enough to gag you. He must have kept it at nearly 100 degrees. His one concession to modernity in his kitchen was the installation of a brick wood box.

Most of what travelling he had ever done was to summertime veteran firemen's musters in neighboring towns, the furthest one being in Portsmouth, New Hampshire, from where he had walked across the bridge to Kittery, Maine. He had, however, once spent a few weeks at some sort of health spa in northern New Jersey, and once he and his father had worked briefly in Neponset, Massachusetts.

Luther was not poor. His lifestyle was of his own choosing. Years of steady work by father and son, and grandfather Luther before that, coupled with extraordinary Yankee parsimony, had gathered considerable substance. The family owned two houses besides the one they lived in. Folks seemed to feel that following the old man's death "young Luther" was worth a tidy sum. However, you'd never know it to look at him. He wore work clothes seven days a week, with rubber boots in warm weather and "felts" in cold. Felts were a type of countryman's foot gear having heavy rubber bottoms and thick felt uppers into which pants or overalls were tucked. He put these on in the fall and took them off in the spring. He did have a seedy blue suit, which he wore to church and funerals with a baseball cap on his head and sneakers instead of the felts. Twice a week, without fail, he came down to the barber shop for a shave.

Mention of the barber shop reminds me of the time he came into the shop in his running pants. Long before it was the rage, Luther decided that it would be a good thing if he got out every day and ran. Inasmuch as common men's underwear shorts were known as "running pants," he felt it would be appropriate to use them for running, so this is just what he did, stopping by Frank's barber shop once for his regular shave. Frank took one look at him attired in his brief gaping garment and instructed him to go home at once and put his pants on and not ever to come into his shop again looking like that.

A very political creature, Luther used to put slogans on the sides of his house. I believe he would have voted for Lucifer himself had he run on the Republican ticket. He told me that in all of his life he had voted for two Democrats: Woodrow Wilson and Al Smith. It was always his custom to occupy a front seat at town meeting from which he could rise and declaim upon whatever article it was that especially merited his attention (much to the delight of the audience). An early proposal to install a public water system brought him to his feet with the exclamation that the whole business was a "damnable perfidious outrage." In his later years this strange but yet engaging little man came to be known to all as "Lootie Toot," a real character.

In the shipyard he kept his own pace. He was a good enough caulker, but nothing could make him hurry. John Prince would become exasperated with him sometimes and make an effort to hustle him up, but nothing John could say made any difference. Luther was his own man and that's all there was to it. When he died, he left several legacies including a trust fund of nearly $150,000 to the town of Essex to be used for the maintenance of the town hall.

With the passing of winter and the arrival of warmer weather, I began to think more of starting up my own yard. I went over there at every opportunity to putter around and take stock of what I would need for equipment. I was determined that our operation would be an improvement over those presently carried on in Essex, and certainly not as primitive as John's. To this end I picked up some power tools and hired an electrical contractor to put in a new and much larger electrical service. Phil Thiel and I cleaned out the old shop and inventoried the existing equipment. Some of that stuff, I think, must have been around from the time my father began there. We put electric lights in the shop for the first time. In celebration of this Margaret and I invited a bunch of friends for a shop party one night. We had quite a time whooping and hollering and running the machinery until suddenly an irate neighbor appeared with blood in his eye. It was obviously time to shut up and go home.

There were a number of salesmen who called at John Prince's yard, some, I think, as much to talk to Old John as to write an order. I remember one in particular, a Mr. Swett, who represented a wholesale lumber firm in Boston. John bought fir from him. Mr. Swett was a fine gentleman, well spoken and always immaculately dressed. After discussing business with John one day, he said to him, "John, I want you to come out to the car with me and meet a friend of my wife's. You know she became a widow a year or two ago and she's got quite a lot of property. I think she'd like to meet a nice man." "Oh," said John, in all seriousness, "I guess I'd better not go out there. I couldn't do anything for her now."

The *St. Peter II* was ready to go by the last week of June. (The reader may notice that it was taking considerably longer to build an Essex vessel than it used to.) She was a good-sized vessel, about 100 feet long with a depth of 11.4 feet. She measured out 142 gross tons. After the experience of January 1944, John put her in a cradle. At that time they had launched the *Gaetano S.* on her side, and she rolled down so far that her raised whaleback bow hooked into the frames of the vessel building alongside and tore down about six of them.

It's a lot of work to build a launching cradle. The ground ways, or tracks, down which the vessel will slide must be carefully placed to be parallel, level crosswise and well supported so that they won't settle. Outboard from the shore, they must not only be well supported, but also secured so that they won't float. This involves driving a great many stakes and placing sandbags, work which must be done at low tide. The sliding ways resemble the runners of a sled and carry the heavy cross timbers that support and carry the vessel. On top of these are the cribbing and shores that hold the vessel upright. Between the sliding ways and the ground ways, like a sandwich, is the layer of heavy yellow grease. The principle of the thing is very simple, but carrying it out is very laborious (and expensive). The two sets of ways are fastened together with bolts at the top and to release the vessel, the sliding ways are simply sawed off behind the bolts, and with no restrictions, the vessel slides down into the water. Care must be taken to ensure that both ways are severed at the same moment, otherwise one side will start to slide before the other, with possible disastrous results, such as befell the *Nat L. Gorton* in 1916. In our case all went well.

Launching day was June 30, 1945, a beautiful hot summer day. The flags were put up, the tide came in, the crowds gathered to watch. The tug arrived and the sponsor smashed her beribboned bottle. *St. Peter II* slid most majestically into the river: a very satisfying experience.

I had decided that with the launching of *St. Peter II* I was going to launch myself into my own business in the shipyard across the creek. And so I did. I thanked John Prince and left to get things underway. As it turned out, John had himself decided it was finally time to retire for good and turn the operation and management of the yard over to Jonathan.

# 6

# Arthur D. Story Shipyard, Inc.

Having now embarked upon my adventure, the first order of business was, obviously, to get a boat to build. I didn't have long to wait or even to exert myself in this direction since the first customer came to me. It seems he had had an interest in a couple of boats that Father built. It was 1945—early in July, as I remember. The war in Europe was over, and it appeared the war in the Pacific would be over soon; already government restrictions on materials were greatly relaxed. The fishing business in Gloucester, and, in fact, everywhere, was booming, and there was an enormous pent-up demand for new vessels.

Benny Curcuru operated the Producers' Fish Company, a large wholesale fish concern that also owned or controlled a number of vessels, and sold ice and fuel oil. He wanted a 100-foot dragger and he wanted a price. A dragger is a fishing boat that drags a large net bag across the ocean floor, scooping up whatever is in the way. Trawler means the same thing. Common usage, however, gave that name to a large dragger. This method of fishing, by 1945, had been used increasingly for about thirty-five years, and wooden draggers had been built in large numbers since the 1920s.

In great elation I set about gathering some figures, and Phil Thiel, working with me now, drew up a set of plans. I had no experience in preparing a cost estimate, but I went at it as best I could, drawing upon my recollections of the stuff that went into a fishing vessel by way of equipment, machinery, and outfit. Some of this, of course, Benny had specified. I had seen a little of this sort of thing at Robinson's since they had taken some fishing vessel contracts before I left. We were to furnish the boat complete except for the main engine and its installation. At length I came up with a figure of something in the order of $58,000. This seemed to be quite satisfactory to Benny, so together with Ed Crowell, his chief bookkeeper, and my lawyer, we drew up a contract.

In addition to a contract, however, Benny, upon Crowell's advice, insisted upon a performance bond. The practical aspects of the performance bond in this case meant that if, for whatever reason, I was unable or unwilling to complete the contract, the bonding company would, itself, do so and then sue me for whatever cost was involved. In any case, Benny was guaranteed to receive his boat for the agreed price.

Although only vaguely understanding the implications of this, I said, "Sure, we'll give you a bond." He suggested I go see his insurance man and have the thing drawn up. Now, of course, no insurance company will write a bond for you unless they're absolutely sure you're good for it, and I was then easily good for it. Upon the death of my mother I had inherited what now amounted to almost one-half of Father's estate, and, with the exception of our house, I blithely proceeded to pledge the whole business as security. This was fine with Benny, so we were off and running.

It occurred to Phil and me that it would be well if we incorporated our business, and so we did, naming it "Arthur D. Story Shipyard, Inc." I was the principal corporator, with Phil putting in a modest sum—what he could afford. I was surprised and pleased that Dick Nielson, an acquaintance from Sun Ship, heard of what we were doing and decided to put in $1,000. He thought it sounded like a good risk.

It was roughly August 1, 1945 that operations really got underway. Manifestly, we had to assemble a gang. In this regard we were fortunate because at that very time the James yard was closed, and the Robinson yard was about to close, so a number of experienced men, especially Essex men, were available. The James yard was closed because it had no work. Its most recent vessel had been completed in April of that year and the last boat it would build was not started until the fall of

1946. At Robinson's yard it was a somewhat different story. Its large program of navy contracts was wholly completed and the fishing vessels with which it "tapered off" were also finished.

Another factor that perhaps had as much to do with the closing of the Robinson shipyard was the fact that the land on which it was built was owned by the Crane family. Mrs. Robinson was the former Florence Crane, daughter of Richard T. Crane, the bathroom fixture magnate. It appears that relationship between the Cranes and Robinson deteriorated to the point where they were anxious to be rid of him. Once he had moved his business to Gloucester, all vestiges of the enterprise, excepting the wharf, were removed and the land restored to its prior state.

My friend Pete Cogswell from the mold loft in Ipswich was the first to join up, and at once he set about doing the lofting and making templates or molds for all of the timbers, using the plans now completed by Phil. I vividly remember discussing all of this with Pete—plans and specs spread all over our dining room table—when word came of the dropping of the first atom bomb on August 6.

The only place Pete and I could find to do our lofting was a building that was part of my father-in-law's property. It was a low rectangular building, about thirty by forty-five feet, having an unobstructed floor. It was very old, having been used in colonial times for the manufacture of malt. Naturally, it was (and still is) known as the Malt House. Although the floor was rough, we covered it with plywood, which was OK, but it wasn't as long as we would have liked. Drawing upon his excellent experience and ingenuity, Pete divided the lines drawing into three parts and laid these down on top of one another. To the casual observer it looked like a plate of spaghetti, but Pete handled it with no trouble.

Perhaps I should pause here to explain what Pete was doing. Briefly, as I said earlier, the building of ships requires templates or molds to be made of each piece of the structure including, for the sawn-frame boats we were building, a mold of each frame. To do this requires that the form of the ship itself be delineated full size on the floor and so, also, each piece. The practical aspects of this preclude having a floor as long as the ship, so the lines drawings that determine the shape must be laid down in sections, one on top of another. In our case, for a vessel 100 feet long, the three sections were about 40 feet, allowing for overlap.

For many years the lofting for all Essex yards had been done by Archer B. Poland in his loft on School Street, South Essex. As a boy, I was delighted to go with Father when he went to inspect Archie's progress on the molds for a particular vessel or perhaps to bring back a bundle of them. Archie's working surface was a kind of heavy gray paper, which wrinkled greatly in damp weather. The actual change in dimensions as a result must surely have been measurable. I particularly remember the carpet slippers he wore as he worked. In those days molds were made from thin pine boards neatly scarfed together, rather than the plywood we used in later years. After use, the molds for a given vessel were neatly bundled up and stored away somewhere for possible future use. Archie was long gone by now, and his loft had been torn down, so in later years a variety of buildings, mostly barns, were used by Essex yards.

To an accountant, the sketchy and haphazard way my father and, I'm sure, many Essex builders kept books and records was appalling. Alone, I think, among Essex yards, the James yard had hired a full-time bookkeeper. Much of their work was done on a time and materials basis. With this in mind, I resolved that I would have somebody to set up and keep a set of books, and I hired Jeremiah F. Hassett to do the job. Jerry had worked in the bookkeeping department at Robinson's, and for as long as I worked there he and Pete Cogswell and I shared our rides to work. Jerry lived at one end of my street and Pete lived at the other.

Again, pursuant to my determination to do things better and more efficiently, I bought a lot of tools and equipment to help things along. The partial liquidation of the Robinson yard made a wealth of stuff available at very reasonable cost. I got a thirty-six-foot steam box (for which I had to buy a boiler), a sixty-foot wooden derrick pole, a crane truck with a twenty-foot boom capable of lifting two tons, a variety of portable electric tools, a mess of clamps, etc., and hundreds of feet of miscellaneous power cords. From the liquidation auction of a yard in Quincy, I acquired a magnificent forty-inch tilting arbor band saw and a fifteen-horsepower motor to go with it.

Nothing like this had ever been seen in Essex before. Our yards had always used the old-fashioned man-killing tilting table saws. I already owned one of these along with a small surface planer, a heavy-duty table saw with jointer, and the crudest trunnel lathe of any Essex yard. These last came with the shop when I bought it, which, by the way, was just as it was when I was a kid. Brother Jake had built a lean-to shed on the side to house the band saw and planer, but the shop itself was the same. To make way for my new saw, I moved the old one to a smaller structure of its own near the timber field.

Of course, we needed an office—there had to be a desk for Jerry, a desk for me, and a drawing board. We took what had been the room with a stove and the paint room next to it and combined them, making a dandy office the whole length of the shop. And for the first time in history, the Story shipyard had a telephone! We built a separate little building for a paint locker out in the yard, along with a spanking new four-holer privy.

I cannot mention that four holer without recalling the time that a salesman got stuck in it. The thing was built with four individual compartments, each having a door that opened inward. There wasn't much clearance between the door and the seat. This particular salesman was a person of large dimensions who, as he tried to enter one of the narrow cubicles, became jammed between door and seat. He had to holler for someone to come and rescue him.

While working for John Prince, I resolved that in my yard the gang wouldn't be lugging eight-inch deck beams on their backs up a long brow to the deck. It was with this resolve that I bought the sixty-foot derrick pole. Along about the last of October we got it set up between the first two ways. (We would eventually have four ways.) It had a long wooden boom that would reach over both vessels. We cobbled up a homemade winch for it, and the whole rig fulfilled our every expectation. It worked so well that, in October of 1946, we set up another one between the other pair of ways. This one was of steel, a former Liberty ship cargo boom, and was more rugged. We supported the wooden one with guy wires strung off the trees and a couple of deadmen; the steel one had supporting legs of T-bar hitched to steel deadmen buried in concrete.

The guy who set up these derricks for us was "Pop" Brooks, an ex-navy man who had been the boss rigger at Robinson's. Pop (nobody in recent memory had ever known him by any other name, and I don't know his real name even now) was as rough and tough and salty a character as one would ever meet. His makeup seemed to embody a steel spring, and he had an enormous capacity for alcohol. At Robinson's it was Pop who moved anything heavy or bulky, things like main engines, tanks, and auxiliaries. We built fifty-foot landing craft upside down on the assembly line, and at the end of the line, Pop picked them up and rolled them over. Drunk enough to require support, he could still turn those things over and never crack an egg. I don't recall that he ever suffered a mishap. His skill was the only reason they tolerated him. Anyway, Pop came to our yard and stood up that sixty-foot pole and rigged it off without batting an eye. It was he who designed, constructed, and then erected our steel pole. This was only fifty-five feet tall. Everybody liked Pop, character that he was, and he was always ready with a favor whenever one was needed.

In fairly short order we had the makings of a good gang. By Christmas that year there were thirty of us, nine of whom had worked for Father or Everett James. Several more were men of good shipyard experience—either in Essex or at Robinson's. One of our "charter members" was an unusual—I might say intriguing—man, to say the least. He hadn't worked for Father or Everett James, but he had worked for my brother Jake and also for Lyman James and John Prince. He was primarily a sawyer and his name was Robert Louis D'Entremont, or more commonly, Bob D'Ent, the son of Liboire D'Entremont, Father's sawyer. Quite bluntly, in the minds of everyone, he was the town drunk. I knew him to be an excellent worker when sober, a man who prided himself on his work and who would give a good day's work for a day's pay. Though his specialty was the band saw, he would willingly do whatever was asked of him and, except for one notable instance, do it well. The incident I mention very nearly had disastrous results for us, but I will speak of that later. Generally, if he'd been drinking heavily, he simply wouldn't show up, nor would he drink on the job, although he once told me that even when "sober" he drank a quart of hard liquor a day. I took that with a couple of grains of salt.

Bob wanted no part of our big new band saw, so I gave him the responsibility for the old one, which we had set up in the back of the yard. As lord of this little domain, and essentially alone, he turned out an enormous amount of work.

I hadn't really known Bob intimately, but we became good friends. He was one of the best conversationalists I ever encountered. He had never finished high school, but I have been told that while there, he was one of the smartest of his class, even though he never seemed to take a book home. He loved animals, especially horses, and as a young man he had acquired a splendid pair of draft horses. Largely because of his drinking, which began at an early age, he soon lost them, but he often spoke wistfully and pridefully of that pleasant time. Though his lifestyle was not what could be called exemplary, one couldn't help liking the man. As I gave him his pay one week I said, "Bob, what are you going to do with this?" "Oh," said he, "I'm going to invest it in stocks and bonds." "Stocks and bonds?" "Yeah—old stock and bottled in bond!"

Years later they fished his body out of the river one Sunday morning. He appeared to have been the victim of foul play. The authorities never did anything about it. Why bother? He was only Bob D'Ent.

If I couldn't be a war veteran myself, I felt I would like to do something for those who were, and I tried to hire as many fellows coming out of the service as I could. Some of these took easily and rapidly to the work and became good men; others didn't do so well. Ironically, the first man I ever fired was an old-time Essex boatbuilder, a man who must have been in his seventies at the time. Will Ross had actually served a while as yard foreman for Lyman James after John Prince left, with rather melancholy results. I had set him to making the stern-post, a large piece that was to be gotten out of a white oak timber twenty inches by twenty inches by twenty feet long. He got the piece out all right, but then carelessly cut it off a foot too short. It put us in a mess. It wasn't easy to come by a timber that size.

To be talking about timber means to be talking about oak—white oak if we could get it, or a good grade of red oak if not. The whole framework of our boats was oak, and in many cases the planking was too. As mentioned, we used fir for ceiling, white pine for decks, and long leaf yellow pine ("hard pine") and/or oak for planking. Framing timber—four-, five-, six-inch stuff—was relatively easy to obtain in Maine and New Hampshire—even an occasional keel piece—but the really big timbers like that sternpost and long keels, together with three-inch planking, came from West Virginia or the Delaware Water Gap. To get consistently good long three-inch oak planking, we ultimately turned to the Maurice L. Condon Company of White Plains, New York. In those days Mr. Condon himself called at the yard. He was a good and reliable man to deal with. We had tried several other sources of oak with dubious results. His prices weren't cheap—one load was $1,000—but it was worth it to get the good stock. His trucks, with their 5,000-foot loads, would always be waiting for us in the morning. It pleased me, however, that our New Hampshire dealer was a family friend, a man from whom Father had bought for years. Bert Janvrin's and my mother's birthdays coincided, and for a long time the families took turns hosting the celebrations.

With the arrival of the keel stock and some six-inch timber for frames, our first vessel was underway. This vessel, like all our vessels, was to be of double-sawn frame construction, meaning that each frame (or rib) was to be laminated from two layers of six-inch timber. By the first of October the finished keel was in place and three or four frames were standing on it.

There weren't enough of us at that time to just grab them and stand them up as was the usual custom, so we rigged a set of shears and hoisted them in place with block and tackle.

From an emotional standpoint, it wasn't the equal of looking into the hospital nursery at my brand new son; still, the satisfaction of seeing the completion of my first keel was considerable. The keel of a 100-foot dragger is a pretty big thing. Generally speaking, the keel of any vessel is the bottom member of a structural girder formed by the framework of the ship with the deck structure as the top member. The keel is also referred to as the backbone of the ship. Our keel was made up of three layers. The top, called the keel, was twelve inches by fourteen inches; the middle, or false keel, was twelve inches by twelve inches; the bottom, or shoe, was three inches by twelve inches. The pieces of the false keel were assembled with four-foot scarf joints and the keel pieces with six-foot scarves. For ease of construction a keel is built upside down, and when completed it is bodily rolled over and placed on its blocks. This is the time when the second construction payment comes due, the first having been made upon signing the contract. In this case we were eagerly awaiting that payment.

Just about the time we turned the keel, Sam Parisi, also of Gloucester, showed up and said he wanted a vessel like this one only a little shorter. He didn't seem to be fussy about the model and suggested we use the same lines and take out two frames. This was fine with us because it meant we didn't have to get a new set of drawings and could use the same molds again, a good saving in cost. He also wanted a price, and taking his cue from Benny, asked for a performance bond. He accepted my price and the bonding company gladly went along; so there we were with vessel number two. With the signing of another contract we got another payment.

Inasmuch as this vessel was to be essentially the same, we quickly ordered another bunch of the same timber and in short order we had a second keel—and another payment. Damn! This was heady stuff! Since frame spacing for these boats was two feet on centers—as it was for most sawn-frame vessels— we would get a ninety-six-footer by taking out the two middle frames. I might say here that taking out or putting in frames of a given model to get shorter or longer boats had been common practice in Essex and elsewhere for generations.

By the end of November vessel number one was completely framed out and vessel number two had over half her frames standing on the keel. We thought this was good progress, but I remembered that in that same length of time A.D. Story or Everett James would have had a vessel nearly ready to launch. Well, we were trying. We didn't have to try very hard to get orders, however. They came through the door, so to speak. Three fishermen from Boston appeared and wanted a ninety-footer, a boat of lighter construction than the first two, with no whale-back (raised structure at the bow) and rigged to dragnets from one side instead of both. Curiously, all these skippers, including Parisi, seemed to be under the aegis of Benny Curcuru. Perhaps the fact that he was head of the Gloucester bank had something to do with it. In any case, they took their advice from him and wanted a price and a bond—which they got. I confess it's hard to believe, but now, forty-four years later, I had to look up the names of all three men. Two were father and son named Tringali, the third was Salvatore Passanisi.

For this boat we needed a whole new design, which was produced, this time, by Pete Cogswell. In this, he was acting as Lew Story had done for John Prince. She was to have double-sawn four-inch timber and use hard pine plank, spike-fastened. As in the first two vessels, we were to supply all except the main engine and its installation. Now we had three vessels underway. Shortly there would be four.

As I look back upon these events, I can appreciate that we were fortunate to have Lawrence C. "Larry" McEwen as our next customer. Larry was a gentleman, a man of intelligence and integrity, a man with education and experience, and a man who enjoyed a splendid reputation in the business and fishing community of Gloucester. He was principally the regional agent of the Cooper-Bessemer Corporation, manufacturers of large heavy-duty marine diesel engines. He also owned and successfully managed two good-sized draggers.

Larry wanted us to build the hull of his new boat, a finely pro-
portioned and able 110-footer designed by Dwight Simpson.
He did ask us to prepare a price, but he did not ask for a bond,
much to my relief. We were especially pleased that we would
not have to concern ourselves with installing all the outfit. Larry felt, quite rightly, that he could better handle that himself.
He had already named his new boat *Kingfisher*.

With four boats now in progress, it was imperative that I
have a good yard foreman and that's just what I had. As a
young man of nineteen, Albert Doucette had come to work for
my father, but to call him an "old-timer" was something of a
misnomer since he was only forty-one at the time I hired him.
However, he had ended up at Robinson's where his obvious
ability and quality of leadership had at length put him in
charge of construction of the *Emily Brown*, one of the big fishing draggers they were building. Though not one of our "charter members," he had come on with us in February 1946 from
the marine railways of Gloucester, and at once I asked him to
take over. As a foreman, Albert possessed that rare combination of knowledge, ability, experience, and a genial disposition. He could get along well with the men and they respected
him. All this was very important for me since the gang was
getting bigger all the time. Initially, Pete Cogswell had more
or less acted as a foreman, but though he was a smart and able
man, he did not have the temperament to be a leader; and besides, I needed him for other things. In addition to lofting, he
would build all our pilothouses.

The winter of 1945-46 was bad enough, though not unusually severe, as I remember. The work progressed as well as
could be expected, I guess, but in no sense can the level of accomplishment equal that of warm weather. They used to say
in the shipyard that "a man with gloves on is only worth half
as much, and mittens are even worse!" It really slows things
up when one has to stop and shovel out or sweep off, or
worse, to scrape ice before starting work. Happily for me the
weather seemed to break in early March and the snow was
soon gone.

The harsh realities of managing a shipyard with four boats

under way were beginning to be apparent. By July that year our gang numbered forty-two men, enormous by Essex standards, yet there was a paucity of experienced talent. Old-timers who needed to be told only once what to do and who then knew how do it numbered only about a dozen or fifteen. We did have some smart, capable young fellows who were fast learners and who adapted quickly; they were a big help. Others were decent enough workers but took no initiative, and for still others, ours was only a job until they found something else. A few, however, were misfits with a capital M.

An interesting sidelight to all of this was the performance of our older workers. I spoke in chapter 5 about working with Tom Boutchie who, at eighty-one, could put in as good a day's work as any young fellow. The older men I had working for me were the same. The trouble was there weren't enough of them. These fellows would work along steadily all day; they were regular in their habits; they seldom complained; they minded their own business. They weren't used to any frills and they did what was expected of them.

By contrast, many of the younger crowd wouldn't dream of doing something by hand if there was a power tool to do it. They'd spend fifteen minutes looking for a Skilsaw and cord when the job could have been done in less than five with a handsaw. It was important for them to keep track of the time; too often they could never be found when you wanted them. As one of our skippers so aptly described it, "They were like a fart in a gale of wind." Theirs was a different work ethic.

Although the coffee break had not become the ubiquitous institution it was to be in the American workplace, we found that willy-nilly we were forced into it. So many of the young guys were sneaking up street for snacks that, in self-defense, we took the pragmatic approach and scheduled a fifteen-minute break at 9:30 each morning.

If I keep harking back to the older men, I'm sure the reader can understand why. For example, I spoke about how, as a kid, I was afraid to go near Walter Cox's planking gang when they were putting on two streaks a day. I found out later that one of the incentives for doing this might have been the promise of a healthy tip from the skipper if he could get the vessel planked by a certain date. Regardless of the motive, he did it, and his work was one of the reasons Father's yard could turn out a vessel in less than three months.

You talk about working—back in those days Walter would give a price for wedging all the trunnels of a vessel, and to do it he would come back to the yard at night after supper and work by the light of a kerosene lantern. It's a wonder he didn't set the place afire.

Walter was working for us now doing our planking and other things as well. He was still a bull of a man with a short temper who didn't suffer fools gladly. If he had had some of his old mates with him, he could still have put on two streaks a day. Back in Father's yard, and now with us, he was also a good one on the framing stage, banging the big frames together in jig time. The young fellows we assigned to work with him were kept hopping, and they also kept a wary eye on him, remembering, I expect, the stories they had heard from other old-timers of how, when he got mad, he would pick up one of the big screw clamps and hurl it clear across the stage.

Walter had a propensity for borrowing a few dollars each week in anticipation of his pay envelope. Also, it didn't take him long to exhaust the contents of the envelope. I remember he called me one Saturday noon from Gloucester to see if he could come to the house to make a small "touch." I could tell from the background noise that he was in a bar room, and when I demurred, he assured me that he wasn't drunk. I was still doubtful so he must have turned and hollered to someone behind him, "Hey, Mike, come here and tell Dana I ain't drunk!" My answer was still no.

A Canadian by birth, he had been in this country for much of his life, although it was not until he was working for us that he applied for naturalization. At his naturalization hearing, I appeared in court for him as a character witness, swallowing hard as I answered some of the questions. Interestingly, I myself had worked with Walter while a member of John Prince's gang.

Two of the best of the younger fellows were John Allen and

Leo Doyle, both of whom came to us on their discharge from the service. John had had a bayonet stuck into his backsides in the Normandy invasion; Leo had served in the Pacific.

There are two procedures of absolutely vital importance in building a sawn-frame vessel: one is molding timber and the other is lining plank. It is the job of a molder to select appropriate timbers from the pile to make the futtocks (component parts) of a frame and to delineate upon them the exact shape of the frame, traced from the mold made in the mold loft. In doing this he must effect an economy of stock, whenever possible taking advantage of any natural crooks or bends. Considering, as I have said earlier, that a large frame may have as many as sixteen futtocks and that a good framing gang can put together five or six frames a day, it is obvious the molder can't let any grass grow under his feet—Remember Uncle Eddie?

John Allen became a good molder of timber. Parenthetically, I might say that initially Phil Thiel molded timber in our yard. He'd never done it before either, but Pete showed him the principles of the thing and seemingly at once he had mastered the process.

Lining plank is in somewhat the same category as molding timber. The liner lays out each streak of plank on the frames of the boat and, through some rather involved and complex numerical processes, transfers the shape of the intended plank to the actual pieces of lumber. Suffice it to say that the whole procedure involves a high degree of skill. The ease and rapidity with which a plank goes on, and the appearance of the whole boat afterward, depend in large measure on the skill of the liner. One man who tried it for us got his streak's edge so far out of whack that he had planks that looked like a snake that had swallowed a goat. Leo was good. He had what one might call a good spatial sense. He took to the job like a duck to water and ended up lining plank for six of the boats we built. Leo, I might add, was a member of one of four father-and-son teams we had. Albert was another. All of them were good men.

It was on a Sunday morning in the spring of 1946 that a representative of the U.S. State Department showed up in town. Howard Southgate had come to discuss with Jonathan and me the possibility of making a film. It was felt that this film would be an instrument of propaganda to be directed at certain European nations in those years just after World War II. In portraying the life of a small New England town as it revolved about a particular industry, it was hoped that it would help to dissuade those nations from turning to Communism. Mr. Southgate felt that our town with its shipyards would be just the ticket. Both Jonathan and I were interested and sympathetic, so right away a camera crew arrived to begin shooting. They worked for much of that spring and into the summer shooting every aspect of shipyard work, and also many aspects of community life. The whole thing was distilled into a splendid little portrait of Essex, its shipyards and its people. Though, as might be imagined, considerable artistic license was taken to enhance the telling of the story (music, singing, and dancing), on the whole the film was a beautiful glimpse of Essex shipbuilding as it was carried on its last years; an emotionally poignant reminiscence of scenes and people now long gone.

Because it's easier for me and for the reader, too, I will henceforth designate the boats by the names they were to receive. Benny's was to become *Benjamin C.*, Sam Parisi's was to be *St. Nicholas*, and boat number three, *Famiglia II*. Larry McEwen's, you remember, was *Kingfisher*. A photograph of the yard, taken on May 20, 1946, shows *Kingfisher* with all square frames in place; *Famiglia II* all framed except for a few after cants and the stern circle; *Benjamin C.*. nearly complete; and *St. Nicholas* all framed and about half planked.

As launching time drew near Benny spent more and more time roosting in our office, a not-so-subtle way of putting the pressure on. I certainly can't say that to date he had been a bother; rather he had become something of a social visitor, as well as just coming over to watch the progress of his boat. He seemed to enjoy sitting in the office conversing with Jerry Hasset or me. We learned a little of his most remarkable career. His was the quintessential "rags to riches" story. Born in Terrasoni, Sicily, he had come to this country in 1900 at the age of eleven. His original intent was to find his father, who earlier had come to Boston in the hope of earning enough money to send for his family. Benny first worked in the mills of Lawrence, Massachusetts, for $4.40 a week, augmenting his income by fishing from a dory in Boston Harbor during the summer. From such humble beginnings he rose to become one of the leading fish buyers on the East Coast, operating three fish businesses and having a financial interest in twenty fishing vessels. His family numbered eleven children. All this was in addition to being president of the Gloucester National Bank. It was under Benny's auspices that our other customers, excepting Larry McEwen, had come to us. As things developed, there would be two more.

Besides his business interests, Benny was a great "joiner." He belonged to the Rotary, the Moose, the Elks, the Redmen, and the Knights of Columbus, to say nothing of being a trustee of Gloucester's Addison Gilbert Hospital. Earlier that spring he had strongly urged me to join the Rotary Club. Foolish though it was, I did, and found myself hobnobbing with all Gloucester's establishment types every Monday noon. They even had me playing my accordian in the club's orchestra. As the Monday's went by, I began to regard the strained affability, the rituals, and the pious mouthings as slightly silly, and when I found myself being fined ten cents for calling men old enough to be my grandfather "Mister," I quit.

Anyway, Albert and I decided we'd like to get rid of Benny as well as the boat, so we put as many men as possible on the job. The *Benjamin C.* was to be a boat for Benny's son-in-law, Joe Ciaramitaro, who was to go skipper in her. Joe, too, would come to the yard every time he was in from fishing, and he was a difficult and unpleasant man to deal with—all the more reason to hurry things up. We couldn't leave the other three vessels unmanned, of course, or there'd be hell to pay, although, in effect, that's about what we did.

By the end of June the *Benjamin C.* was ready to launch. A good spring tide came about 11:00 A.M. on the twenty-seventh, so we planned it for then. I chickened out on putting her over on her side, so we put a regular cradle under her; too bad, too, since launching her on her side could have been done with less than half the labor and one-third the stock. Launching day dawned clear and hot, the dawn finding us down at the outboard end of the launch ways applying the paraffin and grease, and rechecking stakes and sandbags to be sure the ways wouldn't float. With the assurance that the tug was on the way, we began to knock out the blocks, transferring the weight of the vessel to the cradle. In the midst of this my cousin Lyndon Story, one of our gang, came up to whisper that the ways were settling on the starboard side. "You better come!" I rushed to look and, sure enough, they were. Still, it didn't look too alarming; I didn't think they could settle any more. At this point the only thing to do was to get her over as quickly as possible, so we attacked the rest of the blocks with might and main. The way ends were severed in harmony and away went the *Benjamin C.*— a beautiful launching, my first. In Shakespeare's *Julius Caesar*, act 2, scene 2, he writes, "Cowards die many times before their deaths; the valiant never taste of death but once." For whatever you want to make of it, I died a thousand deaths that morning.

It seems that the gang (and others) had come to work that day well prepared to celebrate, and celebrate they did. The libations flowed so freely that some of them even ended up in swimming. Albert and I decided the rest of the day would be a total loss as far as any productive work was concerned so we called the whole thing off.

One of our men who had recently been discharged from the navy was a boyhood chum from Winthrop Street and had come on with us to get his feet on the ground, so to speak. Lieutenant Harry Wood had been a dive-bomber pilot in the navy, flying from carriers in the Pacific. A graduate of Brown University, he was headed for bigger things, but was pleased to spend a few months with us. He was a good man, too—a hard worker. He didn't drink and neither did I, and we thought it would be fun, in view of the circumstances, to go for a plane ride, so we went to the Beverly airport and hired a Piper Cub. Now, here was a man who had had extensive combat experience under the most exacting conditions flying some of our most sophisticated aircraft, yet before he could take up that Cub, he was required to make three trial take-offs and landings to prove he could do it.  His performance was satisfactory, and Harry and I spent a most pleasant afternoon cruising over the countryside.  We flew down over the yard, of course, and saw below us a large load of lumber being delivered with nobody there to receive it.  Wouldn't you know: they dumped it in the wrong place.

# 7

# How to Snatch Defeat from the Jaws of Certain Victory

## Part 1

With the *Benjamin C.* overboard and gone, it was high time to turn our attention to making some real progress on the three vessels remaining in the yard. The owners of these boats had been patient up to a point, but by now what patience they may have had was wearing pretty thin, and I couldn't say I blamed them. We had laid the keel of the *St. Nicholas*, for example, the first of November and here it was the first of July and we were just framing the deck. From a time standpoint this was awful. My father and his gang could have built nearly three vessels in that length of time. Fortunately for us, Sam Parisi, her principal owner, was a pleasant man who bore with us, but not so his brother Tom, who had a mean and combative disposition and told us off any time he came to the yard. We hated to see him coming. He never said a pleasant word to us for as long as he was around there. The *Famiglia II*, boat number three, wasn't quite as bad. We laid her keel in January and by now she was all framed and the planking was started. The problem here was that she had three owners with whom we had to contend. They came from Boston and would always arrive in a body, which helped a little bit, and, though they didn't come too often, we could never know when they might show up. Human nature being what it is, we sometimes gambled they wouldn't be coming for a little while and borrowed their men for something momentarily more urgent. Sure enough—we'd look up and there they would be, coming into the yard at a moment when nobody (or almost nobody) was working on their boat. It's amazing, when I think of it, how many excuses we could make, the assurances we could give that it wouldn't happen again. There were times later on when, if I saw them first, they wouldn't see me. The trouble here was that poor Jerry Hassett and Albert had to cope with it.

I can't tell exactly from my photographs, but we must have laid the keel of the *Kingfisher* in late March. By July all her square frames were in place and the stem was being erected. Naturally, Larry McEwen was anxious to have his boat as soon as possible, but I must pay tribute to his patience and understanding. Having built vessels before and from his experience in dealing with shipyards, he pretty much knew what to expect and was tolerant of our progress. He was somebody we could talk to.

Though the *Benjamin C.* was gone from the yard, she certainly wasn't gone from our attention. We would shortly find out that the outfitting process was a good deal more aggravating than building a hull. We had taken her to the Robinson Marine Basin in East Gloucester to have this work done. W.A. Robinson had established this enterprise upon the closing of his shipyard in Ipswich. He had purchased the property of the old Booth Fisheries and converted the wharves and buildings into a marine outfitting and repair facility complete with all necessary shops and machinery for piping, machine work, electrical work, and steel fabrication. There was also a carpenter shop. All these had simply been moved from Ipswich along with the fifty-ton stiff-legged crane for lifting main engines.

It was our responsibility to provide fuel tanks of about 6,000 gallons capacity, the auxiliary power unit, all electrical outfit and batteries, and masts and rigging—all of the above to be completely installed. In addition, we provided and installed the various items of fishing gear such as the main trawl winch, four gallows frames, necessary bollards or fairleads for the towing wire, steel stanchions for the checkerboards, and a small electric winch for unloading the fish. Gallows frames were the heavy inverted U-shaped steel members, one forward and one aft, which projected up and over the rails and to which the heavy steel cables from the main winch to the bag or net were rigged. These frames had to sustain the whole force of the dragging operation. Checkerboards were the planks on edge that divided the deck area into a number of approximately square compartments into which the fish from the net were first dumped. Benny supplied the main engine, a forty-ton 400-horsepower Atlas Imperial, together with shaft, bearings and propeller, radio telephone, and all navigational equipment. Power to run the big trawl winch was derived from a power take-off on the forward end of the main engine. The auxiliary power unit was a neat little rig in almost universal use by the fishermen. Called the "Lister," it consisted of a bilge pump, an air compressor (for starting air), and an electric generator, all run by a small one- or two-cylinder diesel engine, and all mounted on a common platform. Lister was the make of the British engine so used.

It can be seen that putting in all these items was no mean job—expensive, too. The Basin handled most of it, to be sure, but the presence of a carpenter from our yard was necessary at all times to assist in fitting the various elements and making shelves or platforms. Pete Cogswell with assistant was there, too, to build the pilothouse. The *Benjamin C.* had a steel trunk cabin aft with the pilothouse on top, but we couldn't put these on until the main engine had been hoisted in. My presence there was necessary at least three times a week. It didn't take long for the facts of life to become apparent: this job was going to cost a hell of a lot more money than we were scheduled to receive.

She was ready to go fishing in about seven weeks, at which time we received our final payment. We reckoned that, in round numbers, *Benjamin C.* had cost us about $25,000 more than we got for her. Interestingly, I think, was the fact that our estimate on hull cost was not too far off; it was the outfitting that did us in. There were three main reasons for this:

1. My own inexperience in estimating;
2. We gave a fixed price based upon estimates given me by subcontractors who then billed time and materials;

3.  The national economy entered almost immediately
    after World War II into a period of unprecedented
    inflation, and we were caught with rapidly spiral-
    ing prices.

At any rate, the *Benjamin C.* proved to be a good boat and immediately began making money hand over fist.

During the summer of 1946 we reached our high-water
mark in employment.  At one point we had some forty-two
men, but it was obvious that a number of them were duds.
Most of these left of their own accord, others were fired.  We
found that a slimmer gang of the best men, young and old,
was more productive.  One, however, who joined us in June,
was a man we welcomed with open arms.  George Story (no
relation) was without doubt one of the best caulkers ever to
put the oakum to an Essex vessel.  He had recently been in the
boatshop at the Charlestown Navy Yard and with the slacken-
ing of work there had decided to "come home."  He had begun
as a caulker in 1922 working for A.D. Story on the racing
schooner *Henry Ford*.  He remained with Father to the end.
George's arrival was most timely, since Charlie Baker and his
son, the caulkers we had who came from Robinson's, decided
to go elsewhere.

Here was a ship's caulker with real panache.  Yes, and he
had the total mastery of his craft to go with it.  Somehow one
doesn't ordinarily think of caulking as a craft, yet when it is
considered thats the work of the caulker keeps wooden ship
afloat, and that there is a right way and a wrong way to fill
seams, butts, corners, and joints of all kinds, and that it takes a
large bagful of irons to do this, to say nothing of the skill and
experience to use each one, it is indeed a craft.  George, in the
tradition of all good craftsmen, took a fierce pride in his work.
He was a ham, too, and delighted in hamming up whatever he
was doing if a stranger happened to be watching. With his
beautiful polished black mesquite mallet and a big quid of tobacco swelling out one cheek, he could put on a good show.
In speaking of his work or about jobs he had done, I noticed
with amusement that he invariably pronounced the word
"caulk" as "cork."  And so, by the way, did many of the old

caulkers. And speaking of shows, he was a showman in many other areas as well. He had a wonderful tenor voice, singing in church choirs and male quartets for years. He could yodel and he could play the cornet, bass horn, banjo, guitar, and piano (the last wholly by ear). As a blackface comedian, he was a fixture in the town's minstrel shows, playing the bones. In addition, he had been a cop and a volunteer fireman in his younger days. George had been one of the men I delighted to watch and talk to as a kid in Father's yard.

He had a considerable stock of homely aphorisms with which he larded his conversation. Any time he referred to something he intended to do he always appended, "if nothing breaks or unties." He said to me once, "Story," (we always called each other Story) "you know there's three ages of man: youth, middle age, and when people start telling you how well you look!" One time a young sport in a rather condescending way was describing his weekend activities to George when he was cut off by George's exclamation, "Look here, young feller, I'm like the button on the backhouse door: I've been around some, too!"

So we were pleased to have him come aboard, knowing the caulking would be well done and done with dispatch. For all of his skill, George was not a temperamental prima donna and was always ready to do anything we asked of him. I can say without hesitation that, as much as any man who worked for us, he did his level best for the good of the yard.

I suppose I must have been in Gloucester since I didn't see this happen, but one sunny and hot early summer day a demonstration of brass or gall occurred in the yard such as one wouldn't believe. An advertising agency must have previously scouted out the place, and on this morning a camera crew showed up along with a couple of luscious models. After setting up the gear, the models climbed up on some staging around the *Kingfisher* and started to take their clothes off! It doesn't take much imagination to know the effect this had on our shipyard gang. To a man, tools were left hanging in the air while they clambered to watch. At the back of the yard, where he happened to be working, Albert was suddenly aware of the silence and came out to discover what was going on.  With a few well-chosen words of a pejorative nature, he sent the crowd packing.  All of this was without the slightest "by your leave."  Whether it was to be an ad for brassieres, panties, or bathing suits, we never knew.

Though there may have been clouds on our horizon, the sun shone for us on July 16 that year when Margaret gave birth to our second son, Dana Bradford.  Happily, again things went well.  Little did we realize that one day he would become the sixth generation of our family to build wooden boats on that spot.

That summer we concentrated on finishing up the *St. Nicholas*.  She was indeed taking far too long.  We tried our best to reward Sam's patience and Tom's impatience, and at the same time bring along *Famiglia II* and *Kingfisher*.  Actually, as a spike-fastened boat planked with 2 1/2-inch hard pine, it was relatively easy to make progress on *Famiglia II*.  She had a ten-inch break in the deck but no whaleback so that, too, made things easier.  Also, she was to have drag gear installed only on the starboard side.  This meant only half the work to install foundations for the heavy gear.  *St. Nicholas*, as a larger and heavier boat, had the full complement of drag gear with all of the heavy structure that went with it.  The specifications for *Kingfisher* called for the heaviest construction.  She had full three-inch hard pine plank, trunnel fastened, and to make things interesting, she had five-inch oak garboards, and a four-inch broad streak (the streak above the garboard).

As it happened, Phil Thiel dealt with that five-inch garboard and four-inch broad.  At one place in the rabbet line where the garboard edge butted into the keel, there was a little swoop, which he carefully lined into the five-inch plank such that it appeared the streak's edge had a hump on it.  When that plank went into the mill to be sawed, the fellows there thought the hump must be a mistake, so they sawed it in a straight line. Poor Phil had to line that plank all over again.

In framing our boats, the big degree band saw proved to be a great advantage over the old tilting table type.  Pete Cogswell was able to pick up from the loft floor the degrees of bevel throughout the length of the frame. These he marked on the molds and the molder then marked them on the timbers. As the timbers were sawed, the angle of the blade could be changed as the cuts were made. The result of all this was a finished frame that needed relatively little dubbing (trimming with the adze) before planking. Some areas needed hardly any dubbing at all. I remember looking at a vessel under construction over in Jonathan's yard at this time on which some of the after cants were almost half dubbed away.

As I recall, it must have been just before *Benjamin C.* was launched that Benny announced plans for a second vessel about the same size and to be built under the same conditions. This one was to be for another of his proteges, Captain Custodio Cecilio. Fortunately for us, we were by then sufficiently aware of economic circumstances that we asked our lawyer to incorporate an escalator clause in the contract. This would give us an extra price allowance to compensate for inflation. Benny was willing to go along with this so, by August, there we were with four boats in progress again. Pete Cogswell designed this one although she resembled *Benjamin C.* in many ways. This vessel number five would become the *Mary and Josephine*.

The *St. Nicholas* was ready to launch by Saturday, November 9, 1946. Although from the same lines as the *Benjamin C.*, she somehow seemed a prettier boat. With her topsides painted light gray with white trim, she presented a fine appearance. She, too, had a steel trunk cabin with the pilothouse on top. We put the trunk on here and, though not finished, the house was all framed out by launching day. As with the *Benjamin C.*, I elected to handle the launching in a cradle. The weather was good that day and the tide was coming fast, so we knew the tug would be on its way up the river. We proceeded to split out the blocks and wedge her onto the cradle, but the Parisi brothers had not yet arrived. I had no desire to let her go until they got there, so we held off, hoping they would come soon, although I couldn't imagine why, after all these months, they would be late for their own launching. Suddenly, Albert came to me to report that cradle and vessel were beginning to slip sideways. The sliding ways was showing two inches over the ground ways and pushing hard on the side ribbands. The possible consequences of this were frightening to contemplate. Sam or no Sam, she had to go, and quick. Johnny Allen and Fred Manthorn grabbed the two-man crosscut saw on the starboard side, and Clayt McKay and I took the port. We sawed like hell, and she was free. I seemed to be aware that out of somewhere, a sponsor appeared and smashed a bottle. How or when she got there, I have no idea. By then I was emotionally drained.

By the grace of God the launching went well and *St. Nicholas* was immediately taken in tow by the Gloucester tug *Mariner*. By launch time the November spring tide was a whopper, with the water all over the marshes. It was good to have the depth, but in a circumstance like that it's very difficult to know where the channel is.

Believe it or not, it is only fairly recently, nearly forty years after the event, that I found out what really happened—why the cradle started to slide sideways. It seems that Bob D'Ent, who had considerable experience setting up launchways, was entrusted with placing the ground ways on one side. This was the time he must have been drinking on the job, and he failed to put sufficient supporting material under his ground ways. When the weight of the vessel came onto the cradle, it started to settle in that area, and being now on the grease, it naturally began to slip sideways. Had an accident happened, it naturally would have been my own fault for neglecting to double check the preparations and for letting Bob perform a job of such importance in the first place.

Again, we took her to the Robinson Basin for the outfitting work. She had been in the yard exactly one year. For all intents and purposes the work to be done at the Basin was a duplicate of that on the *Benjamin C.*, except that by now tempers on both sides were getting a little short. Fishermen, by and large, are pretty good at blowing their stacks, and I was getting better at it, too. I suppose I could have taken some consolation in the fact that financially we were doing much better on this job. Instead of $25,000, we only lost $15,000 this time.

A by-product, as it were, of our presence at the Basin was the discovery of a fine, large, well-lighted and unobstructed room on the second floor. I suppose it must have been used in some sort of fish processing when the place belonged to the Booth Fisheries Company. We saw it as a wonderful place for our lofting and so hired it for that purpose. Pete lofted five boats there. What with his lofting and building pilothouses, he was spending much of his time in Gloucester. This was not always in our best interests because a couple of times he and Bob Mansfield, whom we assigned to work with him, got into the "sauce" and came home really looped. Much to my chagrin, they arrived home one afternoon just as our gang was leaving the yard. Before everybody's face and eyes, they got out of their car and stumbled across the yard to the shop. Pete was not overly popular with the gang, and they were delighted to see this. I, however, was not amused. It didn't happen again. I couldn't help but be reminded of Pete's classic remark, "What's a quart amongst one when they all like it!"

I do not propose to burden the reader (or myself) with all of the trivia of our operations through the fall and winter of 1946-47. The gang, now reduced to about thirty-five to thirty-eight men, was doing a good job. Albert was indeed proving to be an excellent foreman, planning ahead and carefully allocating the various jobs to the men he felt could best handle them. The work proceeded as well as could be expected and, most importantly, I felt the quality of our work was good. I tried not to interfere. It continued to be necessary, however, to make reasonable progress on four boats at once.

For my own part, there were many times when I felt that I had to be in two or three places at once. Aside from the yard, my presence was constantly required in Gloucester, and it fell to me to do all the running around in an effort to obtain the multifarious items of material before we needed them. Though the war had been over for a year and a half, many things were still difficult to find—fastenings of many kinds, for example, and miscellaneous small items of hardware. As an investment, Charlie Fears in Rockport had acquired a small mountain of navy surplus stuff, and many were the hours (as well as the dollars) I spent rummaging through kegs and bins looking for the right bolts, lags, screws, or whatever.

I was a truck driver, too, making many trips to Chelsea to bring back trawl gear or fuel tanks from the New England Trawler Equipment Company. To do this we hired an old Dodge platform truck from the local Gaybrook Garage. In exchange for truck rental, the yard built them a splendid oak body; it outlived the truck. I took it to South Boston once for a load of large fir timbers. With that heavy load on, the old girl was practically dragging her tail on the ground. I gripped the wheel in white-knuckled anxiety all the way through Boston and the Sumner Tunnel, expecting that any moment something would bust or a tire would blow. Nothing happened, but my friends at the garage nearly fainted when they saw what I had on there. It showed you can, indeed, expect a little butter on your pie once in a while.

Psychologists tell us, or so I've read, that the human mind tends to retain the happy or pleasant things in life; that unpleasant things or painful events fade, in time, from memory. I think I can substantiate that thesis with my own experience. I sit here at my desk some forty-three years after the events I am describing and I am amazed at the difficulty I experience in trying to reconstruct what happened to me. The people with whom I had happy or pleasant associations are vivid in my memory. I see them; I hear them speaking; I live again the moments we shared. In contrast, I could not remember, for example, the full names of the three men for whom we built *Famiglia II* and I had to look up the name of the man for whom we built boat number six. I have recalled with relative ease the highlights of my first year and a half of business, but from then on, into 1947 and 1948, it all becomes increasingly blurred as our financial situation steadily and unrelentingly worsened, consuming my attention almost wholly, and a number of concurrent events seemed to be in league to defeat me.

An interesting facet of this premise is illustrated in the manner in which I photographed our work. I have been an amateur and semiprofessional photographer for much of my life, and when we began I set about carefully documenting our operations. I have a voluminous file of photographs for the years 1945 and 1946. As 1947 progresses, however, the volume of pictures grows thinner and thinner until, by 1948, there is only a handful. I mentioned in the preface how a fire destroyed all written record of our yard, but I'm inclined to think I would have deliberately destroyed it all, anyway. I really didn't want to remember it. Be this as it may, I will endeavor as best I can to bring forth the salient aspects and events of the remainder of the period.

# Part 2

I guess that it must have been in the late summer of 1946 that Captain Joe Orlando came with an order for a new boat. To our pleasure, he wanted a small (by our standards) eighty-foot by eighteen-foot flush-deck dragger, and he wanted only a bare hull. She would have four-inch frame timber and two-inch hard pine plank. This was just the sort of vessel it would be almost fun to build, and just the sort of thing we should have been doing from the start. Naturally, he wanted a price, but he was quite willing to accept our escalator clause in his contract. Thus we found ourselves with boat number six. She would become the *Salvatore and Grace*.

Signing up another vessel meant, of course, that we were getting a down payment, as welcome at that point as the flowers of May. Payments for every vessel were designed to come as various stages of completion were reached, e.g., signing the contract; turning the keel; completion of planking; completion of deck; launching; completion of vessel. The problem by now was that payments on one vessel were going to pay the bills of the one (or two) ahead of it. Like Ponzi's scheme, this works only so long as one has new contracts coming in. At some point there has to be a day of reckoning. Ours was a classic case of robbing Peter to pay Paul.

Our payrolls alone were running a little over $2,000 a week, not much by today's standards, but a lot back then. I have a grim recollection of coming into the office one Friday morning as Jerry was making up the payroll for the week—due that afternoon. "Dana," he said, "what are we going to do? We don't have $2,000 in the checkbook!" Sure enough, we didn't. There was barely $1,000 in there. "Well," I thought, "we've just finished the framing on the *Kingfisher*. I'll go and ask Larry for our payment." Just to check, I got out his contract to look at the payment schedule and, to my horror, discovered that his next payment wasn't due until the vessel was planked. What a revolting development that was! "Well, Jerry," said I, "I'll go and ask him for it anyway." I did go; I explained my predicament. He consented to do it and made me out a check for $10,000. What a hell of a way to be doing business.

This episode called attention to a number of things, one of which was Jerry's inadequacy as a person to be keeping track of the finances. He was a fine, conscientious man, as honest as the day is long, and totally devoted to our cause, but he was not an accountant—not a man who could deal with our whole financial picture. He was a very sensitive, I might say soft-hearted person, and I remember coming in to look for him one day but he was nowhere to be seen. I went out to look around the yard and, not finding him, I came back to the office. As I entered the shop, I heard a little noise over in the back and here was Jerry, seated on someone's tool box, weeping his heart out; he was that upset with what he could see happening and filled with remorse at what he perceived to be his share in the responsibility for it. That's devotion.

If nothing in particular stands out in my memory about the winter weather of 1946-47, I guess it couldn't have been especially bad. There was an odd but perhaps humorous incident, however, that does come to mind. It occurred one winter Saturday morning when Albert came looking for Bob D'Ent. He had asked Bob to come in especially to saw out a couple of pieces that he needed in a hurry. Bob was nowhere to be seen, nor were there any footprints in the fresh blanket of snow that had fallen in the night. As he went looking to find where these particular pieces might be, he noticed a curious mound over by the timber pile, which he hadn't seen before. Upon investigation, it turned out to be Bob, sound asleep and completely buried under the snow.

It was imperative that we make all haste to finish *Famiglia II* and *Kingfisher*, and to these two vessels we turned the bulk of our effort. The *Famiglia* was the easier to deal with, being smaller and lighter in every way. She did, however, require the construction of a pilothouse. On the other hand, everything about the *Kingfisher* was large and heavy. Gallows frames, bollards, fairleads, and checkerboards were all of the heaviest construction, requiring heavy foundations to be built into the deck framing. In contradistinction to the usual practice of putting all fuel tanks in the engine room, Larry had two large tanks fitted athwartships aft of the forecastle bulkhead, as well as tanks in the engine room. This gave him a greater total capacity and left more space in the engine room for his auxiliaries; it also made the vessel trim better. We didn't need to be concerned with any deck structure since he had contracted with the Robinson Basin to build his large after deckhouse with pilothouse on top. The whole business would be installed as a unit. Larry chose the more modern ketch rig for his spars rather than the schooner-type configuration used by the Italians.

We supplied masts for all of our vessels. Our spar yard was the area next to Main Street and our sparmaker was Arthur Gates, an absolute master of the sparmaking trade. Art had apprenticed with Charles Hanson Andrews in his Essex spar yard, and after Charlie Hanson died he went into business for himself. He didn't have his own place but, rather, made his masts in whatever shipyard was hiring him.

Our masts were all white pine and came as raw trees anywhere from fifty to sixty feet long, from New Gloucester, Maine. To find trees that are perfectly straight is nearly impossible, though it sometimes happens. Usually, there is a certain amount of sweep, however small, in a stick, and the sparmaker must carefully survey each trunk in order to work it to the greatest advantage. Art would carefully roll the great stick over, imagining, as he did, the completed mast contained therein. After striking his original centerline, he would take broadaxe in hand and proceed to square it up, carefully allowing for the proper taper as he went. Having now a stick square in section, he would hoist it onto some trestles and proceed again, this time to make it octagonal.  From this stage, with drawknife and plane, he took down the corners until the finished round mast appeared.  Art Gates did all of this alone; he did it quickly and he did it well.  His finished surfaces, whether painted or varnished, were as smooth as glass, and the masts could not have been more perfectly round had they been turned on a lathe. I recall an occasion when, after squaring off one side of a big stick with his broad axe, Art discovered a scar inside the stick which must have been made by a bolt of lightning. In all other respects it was a beautiful tree, straight and almost knot-free. He hated to waste it, so he reestablished his center line and taper and started again, and again the scar showed up. With grim determination now, Art laid it all out a third time, and this time he won. The finished mast revealed only the slightest stain where the scar had been. It took a good man to do that.

The work progressed without untoward incident and, by the latter part of March 1947, *Famiglia II* and *Kingfisher* were ready to go.  Theoretically, they could have been launched the same day.  We dealt with *Famiglia* first, putting her over on Saturday, March 22.  Nothing went awry with the launching, but a brisk east wind kept the tug from coming in over the bar, and we had to tie her off in the basin over Sunday.  Fortunately for us, the tug came on Monday and took her away.

On Tuesday, March 25, it was *Kingfisher*'s turn.  We had made certain that there would be no slipups on this one.  With a length of 110 feet and breadth of 24 feet, she weighed well over 200 tons, and we weren't anxious for anything to go wrong.  Nothing did.  She charged down the ways like an angry bull and, though the wind was still east, the tug came back and took *Kingfisher* in tow.  She made a handsome vessel and we were proud of her.  I can't say, however, that we were proud of the fact that both vessels had been in the yard for a year.

For a change we could now devote our attention to two vessels in the yard instead of four.  It certainly made a big difference in the progress we could make.  I would like to report that no extraordinary troubles were to beset us, but such was not to be.  Along in April, I think it was, an accident almost cost a life.  Charlie Conrad was on an upper stage along the starboard side aft on the *Mary and Josephine* boring for trunnels, when the chuck of his boring machine slipped off the augur while being pulled back.  Charlie lost his balance and fell backwards some twelve feet into the shallow water below.  Landing essentially on head and shoulders, he should, by all rhyme and reason, have been killed.  That he wasn't is all the more miraculous when it is considered that he held the boring machine in his hands when he fell and, while the water probably broke his fall to a considerable extent, he was only saved from being electrocuted when he landed by the machine's coming unplugged during the fall.  Some of the gang saw him go and rushed to help him.  Here was a man with unknown injuries and, at the same time, soaking wet; he needed to get to a hospital at once.  Essex had no ambulance then, so we called the Fire Department and the small fire truck came.  We quickly hauled all the hose out onto the ground, put Charlie on a stretcher, and shoved him into the open hose bed.  Some blankets to cover him appeared from somewhere and off they went to the Cable Hospital in Ipswich, about four and a half miles away.  By the grace of God once again,  he was not seriously injured, although he was badly bruised and shaken up.  The hospital staff was more concerned with the extreme case of exposure he got from riding in the back of the fire truck.

I'm tempted to say that anybody but Charlie probably would have been killed by the fall.  Though he was sixty-nine at the time, Charlie was still one of the strongest and most rugged men I ever knew.  Everybody knew him as a strong man, perhaps the strongest man in town.  For many years he had been a dory fisherman on the Grand Banks and had seen crewmates, out on the bowsprit beside him, washed off to their deaths.  He had been a crewman on the schooner *Speculator* at the time she was hove down with crosstrees in the water; he had been swept overboard himself.  When he finally came ashore for good, he became a stone mason and also took up the digging of wells and cesspools by hand—alone.  He had the remarkable ability to divine wells with a forked stick, which he did with the same nonchalance and carefree abandon he displayed in dynamiting ledge. Hard work was integral to his lifestyle. Like so many others, he could turn his hand to other things and do a good job. He had been with us from the start and was one of our best men. Whoever it was who first characterized a "granite-jawed countenance" must have had a man like Charlie in mind. Charlie had given me one of my earliest lessons in civility. As a small boy I stood by a sidewalk downtown one day as he was coming along. "Hello, Charlie," said I. He stopped short, regarded me for a moment and then announced, "Young feller, I have a handle on my name. It's *Mister* Conrad!" I will never forget it, nor will I ever forget his fall.

Another large fly in our ointment just then was having to deal with Captain Cecilio. We thought Joe Ciaramitaro of the *Benjamin C.* was bad, but he was nothing compared to this guy. He was forever finding fault with something or picking flaws in the work. He did all he could to stretch various provisions of the contract to his advantage. If he couldn't be at the yard, he would call Albert on the radiotelephone from sea to discuss something he wanted done. He found a heartcheck in one of the shaft log pieces, and we ended up taking out half the log. Never mind that the log was to have a heavy lead sleeve. That hurt. We learned to grin and bear it—well, at least we bore it.

At some time during that summer, Benny was back, only this time in the person of another son-in-law, Sam Nicastro. He wanted another vessel like *Mary and Josephine*, only with another frame stuck in. As usual, they wanted the turkey with all the fixings. I don't think Benny could have yet been aware of what was happening to us or he wouldn't have been there. I wasn't especially anxious to play another set with him, but I suppose there was always the hope that, knowing what we knew by then and having more vessels to build, we might somehow work ourselves out of our predicament. Anyway, we took the job and signed a contract. Having in mind his previous deals with us, I imagine Benny must have been thinking to himself that he knew a good thing when he saw it.

If that was the case, it wouldn't be long before he would experience some measure of disillusionment. Since payments weren't keeping up with bills, we had earlier been forced to go to the bank (not Benny's bank) for a good-sized loan. The bank we used, the Gloucester Safe Deposit and Trust Company, was one of the banks where Father had once been a director. The vice-president and loan officer I dealt with was a man named Bill Otis, a former Rotary brother. A perusal of my portfolio assured him the collateral was there so we got the loan, but the whole portfolio was pledged as security. Along about now that note came due. We could pay it no more than the man in the moon, so, in essence, there went practically my whole inheritance, down the tube and out into Gloucester Harbor. Father must have rolled over in his grave.

We had the *Mary and Josephine* ready to go on August 21, 1947. Like the rest, we launched her in a cradle. Everything at the shoreward end was fine, but just as she was becoming water-borne either something collapsed underwater or the cradle slipped to the side off the ground ways, and she rolled down to port. Her momentum carried her along and she righted herself with no problem. This circumstance of launching was actually no different from that in a regular side launching. We could have given her a good old Essex side launching and saved ourselves a lot of trouble. The whole event was so quickly over that I didn't have time to think of it at the moment, but her steel trunk cabin with a tall pilothouse on top was only held on temporarily by four small lag bolts, one at each corner. Later I got to thinking, "What if those bolts had let go. The whole schmeer would have gone over the side!" But it didn't.

On the third of September, Margaret and I rejoiced at the birth of our daughter, Christine Margaret. Here was an event wholly separate from the shipyard, vessels, captains, banks, or bonding companies. We tried briefly to direct our attention completely to this lovely new arrival in our family—a respite, as it were, from all of the egregious circumstances surrounding us in the business. Praise the Lord!

In quick succession came another launching. The little *Salvatore and Grace* went overboard on September 13. Thirteen though it was, fortune smiled on us and everything was just dandy. We were sorry, in a way, to see her go. It had been a pleasant experience to build her. Over and over I thought to myself what a pity we couldn't have a few more jobs like this. We didn't have to worry about outfitting her, either, and all of the carpentry work that remained was handled by old Dan Fraser in Gloucester. We were now left with only one vessel in the yard, the *Felicia*.

# 8

# The Bottom

As work began on *Felicia*, things were happening and situations developing that now meld into a sort of mental miasma, to the degree that it is virtually impossible for me in 1989 to assign any proper chronology to the events of the late summer and fall of 1947. One of the first things we had to do, obviously and sadly, was to lay off half our gang. Albert and I attempted to pick out and keep about fifteen or sixteen of the best men and let the others go. That was a hard thing for me to do. Furthermore, alarm bells were going off in the council chambers of the bonding company and, in the interests of saving their own skin, they assigned an auditor to keep watch on what we were doing. Principally, this was because the only money we now had to work with was Benny's money, and the bonding company was charged with guarding his interests. One way of doing this was to require me to get the approval of Carroll K. Steele, his insurance agent, before paying any bills, and to have one of the secretaries countersign all our checks. Benny and Captain Nicastro thought seriously of cancelling the contract to build *Felicia*: fishing was not quite as good as it had been, and prospects in the industry were not as rosy. However, I had his name on a contract and I elected to go ahead with it. In retrospect, of course, I shouldn't have.

The *Mary and Josephine* was being outfitted in Gloucester at this time, so Benny would still come up to the yard occasionally. Before a vessel can receive an official number and put to sea, it must have what used to be called a "Master Carpenter's Certificate" signed by the builder. That same certificate is also required by the bank before it grants a mortgage. In a sense, it's a legal title to the boat and it can be a potent weapon in the hands of a builder when the time comes to settle up. I had signed all the certificates for the other boats without incident, and with *Mary and Josephine* nearly ready to go, Benny came to see me one day to discuss business. In the course of the conversation I gave him to understand that until certain items that I regarded as extras were paid, I was not about to sign his certificate. The result was electric. Livid with rage, he leaped from his chair and rushed out the door. He went off and left his hat. We never saw Benny after that.

The fall of 1947 was the time of the great forest fires that devastated many areas of eastern New England, especially Maine, where the whole village of Day's Mills, including the home and mill of Harold Day, a man who had supplied much of our oak and timber and all of our masts, was destroyed. Here at home, the woods of West Gloucester adjacent to Essex were ablaze, taking away a number of homes and summer cottages. By day we watched the columns of smoke and at night the glow in the sky, wondering all the while when and if parts of our own town would go. A wooden shipyard with its piles of lumber, its chips and sawdust, to say nothing of the vessels themselves, is a veritable tinderbox. A bale of oakum, for instance, is only slightly less flammable than gasoline. All of this was a cause of great anxiety, especially since we could no longer afford insurance.

Way back at the time of our incorporation, one of our closest and most intimate friends had indicated a desire to be one of our corporators. He didn't buy any stock, but he wanted his name on the masthead, so to speak. We were glad to oblige: why not? As the going began to get really rough that fall of 1947, he came to the house one evening. After putting out a smokescreen of high-sounding phrases, he got around to his point. He thought it might be in his own best interests if his name were no longer associated with our endeavor. He felt he should submit his resignation. We were glad to oblige: why not? As he left the house, Margaret and I looked at each other and simultaneously spoke the same words: "The rats are leaving the sinking ship."

Winter followed autumn, and with it came one of the worst periods of weather we had seen in a great many years. While, as I have said, I have no special recollections of the previous two winters, the winter of 1948 is indelibly etched in my memory. Beginning in December it began to snow. From then through February it must have snowed at least twice a week. Times without number we were buried. It was cold, too. The two-foot ice on the river was covered with the smelt-houses of local fishermen. It quickly developed that about a third of our labor costs were going to shovel snow and scrape ice. It was ruinous. Things were bad enough anyway, and now the situation became desperate. A desperate situation called for desperate measures. Albert and I called the gang together one morning and laid the cards on the table. "This is how it is, men," I said. "We can't keep spending all this money to clear snow. We'll have to fold up if we do." At their suggestion, we adopted a plan whereby on their own time all would start first thing in the morning after a storm and work as a team to clear the jobs. That done, we would begin the paid time. I dare say it saved the day for us.

In the midst of all this, Margaret had to go to the hospital for a very serious goiter operation. The thing had been growing for some time and now the growth was close to shutting off her breathing. With two small children at home, plus a new baby, it put things in something of a bind. The hospital was in Salem, about thirteen miles away, and travelling the deeply rutted and ever narrowing roads each night was an onerous experience. To make matters even worse, the only room available to her was the most expensive one in the house. A kind friend took in baby Christine for the duration, and grandmother Bishop looked after the boys. Happily, the operation was successful.

The combination of events and circumstances of the fall and winter were having a telling effect on my own health. In addition to difficulties in sleeping, I grew extremely nervous and developed a serious form of claustrophobia. It got so I could hardly go into a building of any kind, especially the bank. Jerry would have the payroll ready for me early Friday morning, and I would go at once to Gloucester with it. Because the stores and offices would not open until nine, I could always get a parking space directly in front of the bank's front door, and at the moment it opened, I would dart inside and go to the nearest teller's window to get the cash. The moment she passed it to me I would dash back out and into my car once again. If it became necessary to go to my lawyer's office, or into anybody's office, I had a terrible time. I couldn't sit down and would stand all the while I was in there, shifting anxiously from foot to foot while feeling faint and sweating profusely. It was absolutely impossible for me to go into a restaurant, and when I went to church, as I continued to do, I had to sit up in the back corner by the door. Anything I did or any place I went that in any way drew attention to me was almost unbearable. Such a condition, of course, imposed a hardship on Margaret and the family, as well as on me. All of this was exacerbated by the necessity of an OK and a signature from a secretary in that damned insurance office every time we wrote a check. I regarded it as a heinous indignity, to say nothing of the emotional pain of the errand itself.

A cardinal rule of any business in tough shape is to meet the payroll first; whatever is left over is parcelled out to the suppliers. This, by now, was what we were doing. Since the only money we could count on receiving would be the remaining payments on the *Felicia*, the object of my game plan was to finish her up and get her into Benny's hands, thus freeing myself from the clutches of the bonding company. It appeared, however, that in order to squeak by I would have to wrestle up a few more thousands from somewhere or I might as well fall on my sword. The Robinson Basin was threatening to sue me for back bills on the *Mary and Josephine*, and other suppliers and subcontractors had us on a C.O.D. basis. One of the local gas stations shut us off. I had to do something and do it quick.

Swallowing all pride, and mustering every ounce of courage I possibly could, I approached my cousin Richard Story, one of the millionaire cousins (the son of Uncle Lyndon), and asked for a loan of $10,000. I hadn't the remotest idea how I would ever pay it back. He hadn't either, but, in spite of his misgivings, he graciously loaned me $4,000, and as things turned out it made the difference between life and death. It's too bad I couldn't have had some of his business acumen. He had put himself through Harvard, and later earned an MBA from Harvard Business School. He went on to become treasurer of R.H. Macy Company and was, in addition, the owner of considerable real estate in New York, Connecticut, and Rhode Island. It was up to me, now, to apply that cardinal rule.

By March, the weather stopped beating on us and turned into an early spring. Considering the severity of the winter, work on *Felicia* had come along remarkably well. Albert and the boys were doing a good job and building a good vessel. The requirements of construction were about the same as Benny's other boats: nothing unusual. I must say that we were glad Captain Nicastro was a decent and pleasant man to get along with. He didn't make trouble.

By April 24, 1948, the *Felicia* was ready to go. On this fine spring day and the launching process went off perfectly. Well, almost perfectly. In order to check the progress of a vessel once overboard, as I explained in chapter 1, we used to rig up what we called a "drag"—a pile of heavy timber  bound around with a chain and connected to the launching vessel by a heavy hawser. As the vessel approached the opposite bank, the hawser would come taut and start to pull the drag, thus arresting her progress. In our case, the thing worked all right except that the drag fetched up against some timbers in the way and the shock of the hawser coming taut pulled the heavy iron cleat on the whaleback  right out by the roots, taking a piece of the deck with it. We needed that!

The Gloucester tug *Mariner*, which had come for all our other boats, had by now gone out of business, so we had to get Captain Valdemar Bang from East Boston to come for the *Felicia*. Once again, and for the last time, we took a vessel to the Robinson Basin. The *Felicia* would be the last vessel to leave our Story Shipyard; with her departure the yard was empty.

As the *St. Nicholas* had been, the *Felicia* was painted a light gray on the topsides with white trim. A trifle longer than the

*Mary and Josephine,* she had a more graceful look, somehow, and presented a fine appearance when afloat. Once more I can say we were proud of our work. From my point of view, it would have been so much nicer if conditions had been different.

With the vessel in Gloucester it now became a contest, in a sense, to see if we could somehow perform the work required under the contract and do it before the creditors finally caught up to us. To do this required a combination of smooth talk, wheedling, cajoling, and assurances on my part, together with a delicate apportionment of available funds in order to maintain progress. Looked at from any angle, this was a thoroughly repugnant process for me. But, as I saw it, it had to be done. Somehow we did it; somehow the boat was finished; somehow we finally got free of that bonding company.

As if all this were not sufficently agonizing and unpleasant, it now became my duty to perform the saddest task of all—to discharge my gang. At that point, I hit bottom. These men, knowing full well my situation, had stuck by me; they knew that their jobs would run out, but still they continued to do their best and to build a good vessel. To the degree that it was possible for them, they tried to help.

The men dispersed in a number of directions. The oldest, long since past the age of retirement, now did exactly that. Others went to the marine railways in Gloucester; some went into house building, and one, Johnny Allen, went into business for himself. Skeet and Leo Doyle and Albert went to Melanson's boat shop in Gloucester, and George Story went back to the Charlestown Navy Yard. Charlie Conrad resumed his well digging (at age seventy), and Pete Cogswell assumed a sort of semiretirement, picking up odd jobs here and there to augment his Social Security.

I suppose that now, in a way, I was free—but free for what? I was free to deal in whatever way I could with the unpaid bills that remained; I was free to see if there was any way to go about picking up the pieces. I was free to go home to wife and family and try to adopt a lifestyle of near poverty. To my considerable chagrin, I was also free to go to my lawyer and ask him to file for bankruptcy. Failure seemed to be coming quite naturally to me. Maybe my mother's theory about thunder-showers was backward; our "thundershower" was going to hang on until the tide turned to come in—whenever that might be.

# 9

# Post Mortem

In order to show that there can be life after death, and not to leave the reader hanging in air, as it were, allow me to render a very brief synopsis of what ultimately happened. Although not immediately, our tide did turn and slowly began to come back in. There were, however, several years of trials and tribulations for my family and me.

When the figures were all finally in and the costs reckoned up, it appeared we had managed to lose about $100,000. I mentioned earlier that losses on the *Benjamin C.* were about $25,000 and on the *St. Nicholas* about $15,000. We did a little better on the *Famiglia II*, losing only about $10,000. How the rest was apportioned I no longer know or care, except that I seem to recall the *Kingfisher* came close to breaking even, and from a purely bookkeeping standpoint, the *Salvatore and Grace* came out slightly on the plus side.

No doubt the reader who has managed to struggle through thus far has formulated in his own mind the reasons for it all. Let me give my list:

1. The three things I listed early in chapter 6 were most certainly true and received even greater emphasis as time progressed. To remind the reader, I repeat them here: my own inexperience in estimating; my giving a fixed price based on the estimates of subcontractors; the unprecedented inflation of the immediate post-war national economy.
2. Poorly drawn contracts, which, although containing

escalator clauses in the later ones, were still impre-
cise and ambiguous in describing exactly what our
obligations were.

3. Utter lack of any proper cost control and financial
   planning.
4. Taking too many jobs too quickly and before we
   found out what we could do.
5. Contracting for the whole vessel instead of just the
   hulls. We had no business giving prices on somebody else's work, and then having the work done
   in a place eight miles away.
6. Insufficient skilled and experienced men to carry on
   properly an operation of this scope.
7. Finally, and I think most importantly, my own complete innocence in business matters. In plain English, I never had to know the real value of a dollar,
   had never had to struggle to make ends meet. It's
   not necessarily a good thing to be born with a silver
   spoon in one's mouth. The lessons I learned should
   better have been learned much earlier.

We did file for bankruptcy (technically it was labelled re-
ceivership) and at length the shipyard property went up for
auction. Shortly before the time of the auction, nearly two
years later, the old shop and mill caught fire and were almost
totally destroyed. Ironically, the fire made some money available for distribution since my uncle, Burton Adams, horrified
to find out we had no insurance, had taken out a policy and
paid for it himself. We had also sold off some of the equipment. At auction time there was not a lot left around there,
and the real estate was in tough shape. Two loyal and devoted friends were present to bid if necessary and make sure the
place remained in my hands. Actually, very few people were
present and those who were fully understood my situation. As
no one else bid, I bid it in myself on the basis of $96,000 in
notes on the corporation I held.

With the help of God and a wonderful wife and family, we
(no longer the corporate "we") were able, ultimately, to climb

out of our pit and resume a new life. For a time I was forced to take a job as a pick and shovel laborer for the contractor putting in the town's new public water system, and there were occasions when I wasn't sure where our next meal would come from. However, we managed to survive. I did feel bad that several of our suppliers, some of them fine men in little businesses of their own, were burned in our failure; it troubles me to this day, even though they're all dead by now. We went on to turn the property into a boatyard, hauling, storing, and building small wooden boats in a new shop. At length my son Bradford joined me and together we built a good little business. At that point he became the sixth generation of our family, beginning in 1813, to build wooden boats on that spot.

As a postscript to all of this, I can report that all of my boats were good boats; they performed ably and well and they made money—some, very good money—for their owners. This last, of course, is small consolation to me. Benny's boats, the *Benjamin C.*, *Mary and Josephine*, and *Felicia* were sold to Nova Scotia in February 1954 and fished out of Louisburg. They had been very successful fishing out of Gloucester under Joe Ciaramitaro, Chris Cecilio, and Sam Nicastro. They were sold following trouble with the fisherman's union in Gloucester. Knowing Benny as I did, I'm sure he made some money on the deal.

The *St. Nicholas*, under Sam and Tom Parisi, did well until a fire in the engine room spread to the whole boat. She burned and sank near Georges Bank in August of 1963.

Larry McEwein operated the *Kingfisher* for as long as she was profitable. I don't remember what year it was, but he finally sold her, from which point she was held by a number of owners, each of whom allowed her to deteriorate a little more. I think she finally ended up as a pogie boat. I remember going to look at her once as she lay sunk in a dock in Gloucester. Someone had left a valve open. It was a sad sight indeed, and a sad reward for such a proud vessel.

Before she ever went to sea, the name of the *Famiglia II* was changed to *Agatha and Patricia*. She fished out of Boston and Gloucester for many years. The *Salvatore and Grace*, too, was a good little work-a-day vessel out of Gloucester for a long time.

As it turned out, the post-World War II years of 1945 to 1949 were a last hurrah for wooden shipbuilding in Essex, although smaller bent-frame boats continued to be built, and even today a Story is still doing it. It's interesting to note that the winter of 1947 saw three Essex yards in operation: the James yard had one vessel, Jonathan Story had two, and we had four. The *Bright Star* on April 5, 1947 was the last James vessel launched; the *Felicia* on April 24, 1948 was our last; the *Eugenia J.* on June 29, 1949 was Jonathan Story's and the town's last. A beautiful little schooner she was. Nearly 300 years of Essex wooden shipbuilding tradition and our only native industry had come to a close.

As I mentioned in the preface, these years essentially marked the end of wooden shipbuilding country-wide. A few yards persisted along the Maine coast and some in North Carolina and the Gulf area, but these, too, died away in a few years. It had become cheaper, easier, and quicker to build boats of steel.

With the end of shipbuilding, Essex was no longer unique among its neighbors (unless you want to count the clam industry). Like most other places, the town changed, the people changed, the local businesses changed. The old Anglo-Saxon names began to die out and disappear, to be replaced by a potpourri of new ones originating everywhere. The old maxim we found to be true: "The only thing permanent in this world is change."